HANDBOOK OF
SOVIET MUSICIANS

By

PROFESSOR IGOR BOELZA

Edited by ALAN BUSH

GREENWOOD PRESS, PUBLISHERS
WESTPORT, CONNECTICUT

Originally published in 1943
by The Pilot Press Ltd., London

First Greenwood Reprinting 1971

Library of Congress Catalogue Card Number 74-114468

SBN 8371-4764-6

Printed in the United States of America

CONTENTS

★

iii

FOREWORD

★

PROFESSOR IGOR BOELTZA'S *Handbook of Soviet Music* is a compendious up-to-date survey of Soviet concert, operatic, and ballet music. Forty Soviet composers are dealt with individually. This is less than 10 per cent. of the total membership of the Union of Soviet Composers. Nevertheless in this selection are included examples of all the diverse types of composers who are hard at work in the U.S.S.R., producing a vast mass of music.

In addition the complete catalogue of these composers' works gives some indication of the amount and variety of music printed and thus available to the Soviet public. If this handbook does nothing more than stimulate the demand in this country for copies of Soviet musical works it will achieve a useful purpose.

Yet neither the study nor even the performance of the musical scores of Soviet composers, *when considered apart from their context as an integral part of the life of the Soviet people in general,* can bring a full understanding of the significance of Soviet musical development in relation to the history of music as a whole. In the author's introduction, he says something about the assistance which music in general and composers in particular receive from the State; he deals also with the activity of the music-publishing organizations, and touches upon the musical developments of the Autonomous Republics; lastly, he explains the ideas which guide Soviet musical life in general.

For a full appreciation of the importance of the musical developments in the U.S.S.R., however, it is necessary to know in accurate detail the activities of the amateur musical organizations, of the children's musical life, both professional and amateur, and to see clearly the relation between cultural activities—including music—and the social aspects of Soviet life, whether at the

v

demonstrations such as those held on May-Day, at the organization of new enterprises such as the building of the Ferghana Canal, or at the less spectacular but none the less significant seasonal festivities in the life of the collective farmers, or at the periodical occasions which celebrate new peaks of achievement among the industrial workers. More factual information is needed regarding the musical developments of the Autonomous Republics.

The growing friendship between the peoples of Great Britain and the U.S.S.R. stimulates mutual interest in the cultural achievements of both countries, and will no doubt make available the data which are indispensable to complete mutual understanding on both sides. In the meantime, this *Handbook of Soviet Music*, as a factual survey of one important aspect of the subject, brings us a step farther along this road.

ALAN BUSH.

London, May, 1943.

BIOGRAPHICAL NOTE ABOUT THE AUTHOR

★

IGOR FEDOROVICH BOELZA, b. 1904 in Keltzy, Poland, son of a lawyer, received his secondary education in Warsaw and Lubny (Ukraine); later attended the Conservatoire of Kiev; graduated in 1925 having studied composition under Boris Lyatoshinsky; in the same year started his career as a teacher in the Kiev Conservatoire, lecturing on composition and history of music; professor until 1941; 1930–37 was head of the Musical Department of the Kiev Film Studio and professor of the Kiev Institute of Cinematography; since 1938 has been editor of the review *Soviet Music* and in charge of the Ukrainian Musical Publications; moved to Moscow in August, 1941.

His works, which are written in an atonal and polyphonic idiom, include four symphonies, a fifth being in progress, a concerto for pianoforte and orchestra, a concerto for organ, a string quartet, a trio, five sonatas for piano, numerous instrumental pieces and songs, music for films, etc. In addition he has written works on musical research including a monograph on Mozart, a course of lectures on film music, and a study of works by Soviet composers; at present he is writing a book on musical culture in England and in the U.S.A.

INTRODUCTION

★

THIS COLLECTION comprises a series of short articles about forty Soviet composers of Russia, Ukraine, Byelorussia, Georgia, Armenia, and Azerbaijan, ranging from the older masters who started their activity before the October Revolution to representatives of the younger generation of composers who have already grown up in the Soviet era. It does not pretend to be exhaustive, but, insofar as its limits allow, it contains basic information about those composers whose works are most representative of the important characteristics of Soviet music.

The last twenty-five years brought to the peoples of the Soviet Union considerable progress and joyous changes in their lives, which carried with them an extraordinary flourishing of culture and art in all its branches. In the realm of music also this quarter of a century was characterized by interesting developments. Russian classical music was created during the hundred years preceding the October Revolution, and its place in the world has been asserted by Glinka, Dargomizhski, Balakirev, Mussorgsky, Borodin, Chaikovsky, Rimsky-Korsakov, Serov, Rubinstein, Cui, Skriabin, Rachmaninov, and others. But music in Tsarist Russia belonged only to a few. The works of the Russian composers were always inseparably linked with the life, feelings, and aspirations of their own people and its art, the treasures of which have enriched Russian music and have determined its national character. It is, however, only the October Revolution that has made Russian art the property of the whole people. A radical reform of popular education was adopted, particularly in the field of music. Moreover, the creation of numerous theatres, concert organizations, ensembles, circles, professional art organizations— all testify to the government's attitude which has made the development of musical culture in the Union possible.

Already in 1918, at the dawn of the existence of the Soviet

Régime, V. I. Lenin had personally taken part in the solution of many problems affecting the development of art in Russia. To-day, likewise, Joseph Stalin constantly devotes careful attention to these problems.

The development of all art in the Soviet Union rests on a secure material basis. The existence of theatres, conservatoires, philharmonic orchestras, and publishing houses is provided for by the Government. Similar conditions have been created for the Soviet composers who are organized in a professional body—the Union of Soviet Composers of the U.S.S.R.—with branches in the various republics and autonomous regions. Every composer who begins to work on a new composition is allocated a sum of money (determinable by his qualifications and the nature of the proposed work) which is paid out to him in the course of his work. On completion, the new work is discussed in the Union of Composers. Thereafter the author concludes a contract with the concert organizations (philharmonic orchestra, radio, etc.) and the publishing house, the condition being that the fees are paid not only for the right of publication or recital, but for every individual performance. The control of this arrangement is entrusted to a special office for the safeguard of copyright. The radio which receives a government grant plays an important role in the propagation of new works, and a similar grant is allotted to the publishing houses. This course enables the publication of even the most monumental works which, on account of their limited number of copies and the high cost of production, are usually deficit-bearing. This deficit is wholly covered by the government subsidy. One can gain an idea of the amount of such subsidy from the fact that during the last twenty-five years there have been published several thousands of orchestral, choral and chamber music scores of Soviet composers alone, excluding an extensive library of Russian and West-European classical works. Thus the percentage of unpublished compositions (in most cases only early creative attempts) is very small, whereas the published musical output makes it possible to follow the trends of development of Soviet music.

Already in the early post-revolutionary period most of the

Soviet composers began to take an active part in the building up of Soviet musical culture and in its broad democratization. In those years the conservatoire in St. Petersburg was headed by Alexander Glasunov, in Moscow by M. Ippolitov-Ivanov, and in Kiev by R. Glier, each of whom became the centre of groups of teachers, composers, executants and musical scholars. These three oldest masters symbolized the live bond between the heritage of Russian classical music and Soviet music, a bond which is still growing increasingly strong.

Russian classical music has always been characterized by progressive democratic strivings towards national spirit in art, and by philosophical depth and truthfulness, which our generation took over from its great ancestors. The creative quests of Soviet composers, which passed through many contradictory phases, were primarily bound up with the problem of realism in music, to the solution of which every composer has a different approach. Every epoch has its distinct style which is born out of arduous trials, but the meaning of style in the broad sense of the word does not lie in the uniformity of means of expression, thematics and technicalities, but rather in the ideological trend. Therefore, when speaking about the Soviet style I keep in mind above anything else the philosophic and aesthetic conceptions on which it is based. These conceptions are historically bound with universal culture and with the humanitarian ideals of the epochs of Antiquity, the Renaissance, and the subsequent centuries. Real art is always humanitarian. Man is striving towards sunshine, intelligence and happiness; he is fighting for these ideals and, like Mozart's Zarastro, is overcoming all evil forces of the Kingdom of Darkness. The world of human feelings and strivings is a wonderful world, as indeed is human life itself—no less wonderful than death encountered in the struggle for the happiness of mankind. This world is unfolded in the works of art of all great masters of the past and of the present.

History is the judge not of people alone but also of their works and thoughts, as well as of their art. Every immortal work of art is above all truthful. It is not the destiny of every master to be a great and immortal but everyone can be truthful. Precisely the will and striving towards truthfulness have shown the way to the Soviet composers, the way which leads to realism, or—in other words—to the truthful interpretation of the inner world of man in his works of art. This aspiration is at the very basis of Soviet music and is revealed in all its varieties. True, for some time the tendencies of the West-European music of the twenties have influenced the works of many Soviet composers and have left traces still perceptible at present; but these tendencies were primarily due to the desire to achieve a widening of the means of expression and to the search for new methods of emotional effects.

A multitude of creative personalities, schools and movements has been always characteristic of periods of high flourishing in art. This is now taking place in Soviet music which is developing several distinct trends. It is only natural that the older generation of composers should be most intimately linked with the traditions of Russian musical classics; thus in the music of Glier and Steinberg the affinity with the music of Rimsky-Korsakov and Borodin is very marked; in Myaskovsky's music there is a bond with Chaikovsky and Taneev. These affinities are passed on to the subsequent generations as, for example, can be observed in the music of Kabalevsky, Myaskovsky's pupil. But this affinity, in the proper sense of the word, will only come to light if it is a true part of the creative personality of the pupil himself. The most eminent teachers in charge of composition classes are at the same time the leading composers. But never do they exercise any constraint or attempt to alter the individual features or artistic convictions of their pupil. This is eloquently proved by a comparison of the music of Steinberg and that of his pupil Shostakovich; Myaskovsky and his pupils Shebalin and Khachaturian; Glier and his pupil Lyatoshinsky. Similarly, the young composers of the following generation who study under Shostakovich, Shebalin and Lyatoshinsky, represent a great variety of trends.

Folklore elements occupy an important place in Soviet music just as they did in the classical Russian music, beginning with Glinka. They find expression in both a quotational method of the use of folk-song themes and, mainly, in the tonal kinship to popular music; the latter is far more characteristic. Thus, for instance, when speaking about the elements of Russian folklore in Shaporin's music, Armenian in Khachaturian's, Georgian in Muradeli's, Byelorussian in Bogatyrev's—we refer to the composers' creative penetration into the rhythm, the idiom and the visionary world of popular music, and in no way to a direct quotational use of its melodies. With many composers the drawing on folklore is only of an episodical character, but with some (particularly in the quartets of Shebalin) it takes on a peculiar reference to specific idiomatic forms. On the other hand the music of some composers is wholly linked with the folklore of their people. This is the case with the Georgian composer, Kiladze, the Azerbaijan, Gadzhibekov, the Ukrainian, Revutsky, and with others. Nevertheless, the outstanding and original creative personalities of the leading Soviet composers who benefited by the experience of the entire European musical culture and who were able to generalize it synthetically in their own music, exercise a noticeable influence on other Soviet composers. Thus, for instance, the influence of Prokofiev is felt in Polovinkin's and Mossolov's works, and the influence of Shostakovich on the younger generation is increasing daily. The range of expressive means used by the Soviet composers is extremely varied, and the principle adopted for the selection of these means indicates a variety of schools. If we take, for instance, the harmonic language we find a group of masters like Glier, Shaporin, Steinberg and others, whose music is basically built on classical lines, whereas in the works of Myaskovsky and his followers these lines are noticeably sharpened. Still more elaborate combinations are used by Shcherbachev and Alexander Krein, whose harmony has much in common with Skriabin. The music of Prokofiev and Shostakovich is characterized by audacity and innovation in the real of harmony. They trespass the bounds of tonal harmony and use elaborate vertical complexes. Many works by Shebalin, Popov and Lyatoshinsky are planned in atonal harmony, but their atonalism does not take origin in the twelve-tone system of Arnold Schoenberg (which to the best of my knowledge has never

xiii

had any followers in Russia), but evolves from the harmonic principles of Liszt's later creative period.

A similar variety exists also in the melodic and scalic tonal structure of music and in the principles of thematic development and instrumentation.

Here should be noted the enrichment of the experience of Soviet composers through their acquaintance with the mus·c of the various nationaltiies who were given the opportunity after the October Revolution to develop freely their national cultures in a continuous fraternal intercourse with all other peoples of the Soviet Union. And, lastly, we should point out the great abundance of thematics and genres, which is one of the characteristic features of Soviet music. Alongside with operas, ballets and symphonic works on contemporary and historical topics, as well as instrumental, vocal, and chamber music, there grows a cantata-oratorio genre with strivings towards monumentality and broad symphonic development (e.g., Shaporin's symphony-cantata "On the Kulikov Field" and "Alexander Nevsky", Prokofiev's "Zdravitsa", Kabalevsky's cantata "Our Great Fatherland", Koval's oratorio "Yemelian Pugachev"). The song element dominates in this genre; it is equally present in Knipper's symphonies with choir where he makes extensive use of mass songs.

The songs of Soviet composers have grown to be an inseparable part of the people's life. They are heard everywhere—on the front, at military parades, in parks, in factories, in towns and villages, and in the family circle. The whole life of the Soviet people is pervaded with songs which speak of its life and struggle, and which call for victory and happiness.

Now in war time, this call rings with particular vigour and patriotic elation in the works of all Soviet composers. On the occasion of the twenty-fifth anniversary of the October Revolution they have all produced new compositions reflecting the ways of life in their native land, its constructive efforts, and that great struggle which the Soviet people, together with other freedom-loving nations of the world, is carrying on against the mortal enemy of mankind—Fascism.   IGOR BOELZA.

Moscow, 26th August, 1942.

ALEXANDER VASSILYOVICH ALEXANDROV

★

B. 1884 in the village Plahino, near Riazan, of peasant origin; was admitted to the Choir Academy in St. Petersburg from which he graduated as conductor; simultaneously studied theory of composition in the Conservatoire under Rimsky-Korsakov and Glazunov; graduated with distinction from the Moscow Conservatoire in 1933, where he studied composition under Sergie Vassilyenko and singing under Professor Mazetti; started teaching in the old Russian city of Tver (now Kalinin); is now professor at Moscow Conservatoire.

He is both composer and conductor. From 1926–30 he was conductor of the Moscow State Choir, and subsequently—from 1928—conductor and art director of the famous "Red Banner" Ensemble of Red Army Songs and Dances of the U.S.S.R. He received the Order of the Red Star in 1935, the Order of the Red Banner in 1939, and the title of People's Artist of the U.S.S.R. in 1937, and was awarded the *honorary degree of doctor of sciences* research in art) in 1939.

The first battle song of the war sung by the whole Soviet populace was his "Patriotic War".

1

ANATOLE NIKOLAEVICH ALEXANDROV

★

B. 1888 in Moscow, son of a teacher; learnt the piano and started to compose at the age of eight; studied composition under Taneev; entered Moscow Conservatoire in 1909; studied pianoforte under Igumnov and Vilshaw, and composition under Vassilyenko and Ilyinsky; on graduation was awarded the Gold Medal; now a composer and professor of composition at the Moscow Conservatoire; awarded the degree of Doctor of Science (research in art) in 1941. He has studied Kabardino-Balkarian folk themes, making them the basis for several orchestral works. He has also arranged folk tunes of Western Europe, including English folksongs.

BORIS VLADIMIROVICH ASSAFIEV

★

B. 1884 in St. Petersburg; studied philology at St. Petersburg University; took his degree in 1908; then entered the Conservatoire, studying composition under Lyadoff. Is both composer and writer on music under the pseudonym "Igor Glebov"; now professor at the Leningrad Conservatoire and head of the Musical Section of the Institute of the History of Art; he has written books on Chaikovsky, Glinka, Stravinsky, Skriabin, musical form, etc., and music for the theatre, a series of ballets on themes by Pushkin, Lermontov, and Balzac, as well as symphonies, operas and other works.

He has received the Order of the Red Banner and the title of People's Artist of the R.S.F.S.R. In 1940 he was awarded the degree of Doctor of Science (research in art).

During the first year of war he wrote among other works two symphonies, the "Suvorov" suite for brass orchestra, and books on Liszt, Glinka, Czech music, and other monographs and research works.

VICTOR A. BELY

★

B. 1904, son of a doctor in the Ukrainian town of Berdichev; at the age of eight played the violin and mandolin; later learned the viola and played in the local amateur quartet; taught himself in addition the piano. At twelve lost his father on the Russo-German front; 1919 entered Kharkov Conservatoire, studying violin, in 1921 composition; 1922 entered Moscow Conservatoire, studying composition under Konius and Myakovsky; graduated in 1929, his name being engraved on the golden panel; his diploma work was a long suite for choir and orchestra in four parts; now a professor at the Moscow Conservatoire.

He has devoted much time to the study of folk songs and produced suite for choir on Chuvash themes, a cycle of Chuvash songs, and piano miniatures on Bashkirian themes. Whilst his early compositions bear the influence of Skriabin and Ravel, and his sonatas for piano indicated that he was not free from expressionist influences, his later compositions mark a clarification of style and an inclination towards the national spirit, particularly in his vocal works. This is true of many of his songs written before the war, such as the "Eaglet", but particularly of those written during the war: "The Song of the Brave", a battle song of the Red Army; the "Ballad of Captain Castello", extolling the legendary deed of the Soviet flier; the "Slav Suite" for choir à capella; the song "Partisans in the Woods", and many others.

Besides composing, he writes articles, and is now a member of the Presidium and leader of the Defence Section of the Organizing Committee of the Union of Soviet Composers.

He has written many battle songs, and for the occasion of the twenty-fifth anniversary of the October Revolution he produced an oratorio on the theme of the twenty-eight guardsmen who met their heroic death in unequal battle with fifty German tanks during the approach to Moscow in 1941.

4

ANATOLE V. BOGATYREV

★

B. 1913, in Vitebsk, Byelorussia, son of a teacher of languages; began to learn music at eight; entered the Vitebsk Musical School in 1929; in the following year entered the Minsk School of Music, and in 1932 when a State Conservatoire was opened in Minsk (capital of Byelorussia), was admitted into the composition class of the theoretician and composer Vassily Zolotarev, a pupil of Rimsky-Korsakov; in 1937 completed his diploma work, "Poem on the Tale of a Bear" (after Alexander Pushkin) for choir, soloists and orchestra; at the same time studied Byelorussian folklore and produced a series of arrangements of Byelorussian popular songs; 1940 was awarded the Order of the Red Banner, and in the next year won the Stalin prize for his opera, *In the Thick Woods of Polesye.*

In the first months of war he produced a cantata "To the people of Leningrad", a number of war songs, and music to the play by Romashev "Stars Cannot be Dimmed", about the autumn battles on the approaches to Moscow. He is now working in Sverdlovsk, where he continues to discharge his duties as deputy to the Supreme Soviet of the Byelorussian Soviet Socialist Republic (to which he was elected in 1938) and deputy-director of the Conservatoire.

ISAAC O. DUNAYEVSKY

★

B. 1900 in Lokhvitsi, near Poltava, Ukraine; 1910 entered the Kharkov Musical School where he studied violin under Joseph Akhron; during this period started to study theory of music under Simon Bogatyrev; graduated 1919 from the Kharkov Conservatoire; wrote music for theatres of Leningrad, Moscow and Kharkov; later wrote his first operettas; was one of the first composers in the U.S.S.R. to start using jazz (1933); wrote music for many films, including "The Merry Boys" and "Circus"; the "Song of the Fatherland" from "Circus" is his most popular work.

Simultaneously with his film music he wrote new operettas: "The Golden Valley" and "The Road to Happiness", numerous songs and choruses, among them "Song of Stalin" for choir and orchestra.

He is not an innovator in music. He is mainly concerned with making his music comprehensible and accessible to the masses, and attains great expressiveness by means of simple and tested methods. The source of his success lies in the lyrical melodiousness of songs on themes near to the people's heart and familiar to them. Hence also the popularity of his patriotic songs whose contents is so moving and so well understood by everybody.

In 1936 he was awarded the Order of the Red Workers' Banner and the title of "Merited Artist of the U.S.S.R.".

IVAN I. DZERZHINSKY

★

B. 1909 in Tambov; entered Gnessin Musical School in Moscow in 1928; two years later studied in the Leningrad Conservatoire under Professor Ryazanov; after leaving the Conservatoire was greatly helped by Boris Assafiev and Dmitri Shostakovich; to the latter is dedicated his opera *Quiet Flows the Don*.

His operas, *Quiet Flows the Don*, completed in 1934, and *Virgin Soil Upturned*, published in 1937, are both written after the novels of Michael Sholokhov.

His next opera, *In the Days of Volochayev*, was also inspired by events of the recent past, the heroic days of civil war in the Far East. His fourth opera, finished only a short time ago, is written to a libretto after the well-known drama of the Russian playwright, Alexander Ostrovsky, *The Storm*. In the first months of the war he wrote a one-act opera, *The Blood of the People*, whose subject is guerilla warfare.

Has been awarded the Order of Lenin.

UZEIR-ABDUL-HUSSEIN-OGLI GADZHIBEKOV

★

B. 1885 in the village of Aghzabed, Karabi, in Azerbaidan; after passing through a Russo-Tartar school, entered teachers' training college in the Georgian village Gori—the birthplace of Stalin—received there a theoretical introduction to music and was taught to play violin, violoncello and wind instruments.

While studying in the college resolved to devote himself wholly to music; studied popular Azerbaijan music, worked intensively on the theory of composition, both in Baku (1904–11) and later in Moscow and in St. Petersburg. Financial difficulties prevented completion of his studies in the St. Petersburg Conservatoire where he worked under Professor Calafati.

The October Revolution opened unheard of possibilities for the development of national cultures in the Soviet Union, and from that time on he could devote himself wholly to the Azerbaijan music. He was directly responsible for the drive for organization among Azerbaijan composers. Became the head of the newly-opened Azerbaijan Conservatoire in Baku and conductor of the choir of the State Philharmonic orchestra. He has published a collection of songs, a treatise on popular Azerbaijan music, and various text books and manuals; in addition he has devoted much time to the education of young composers.

He is the creator of the Azerbaijan National Opera, beginning his career as a composer thirty-five years ago, when his first opera, *Leili and Medjnun*, appeared in 1907; since then he has produced ten musical dramatic works of the most different kinds, ranging from the heroic *Ker-Ogly*, for which he was awarded the Stalin Prize for 1941, to the musical comedy, *Arshin-Mal-Allan*.

He has been awarded the Order of Lenin and the title of People's Artist of the U.S.S.R.

8

REINHOLD M. GLIER

★

B. 1875 in Kiev, son of a maker of wind instruments; learned the violin as a child; before long started composing music which was played in his father's house, a meeting place for many musicians; 1891 entered the Kiev Musical School where he stayed for three years studying violin and composition; 1894 was admitted into the Moscow Conservatoire and studied violin under Professors Sokolovsky and Grgimali, harmony under Arensky and Konius, counterpoint under Taneev, composition and instrumentation under M. Ippolitov-Ivanov; 1900 graduated from the Conservatoire with his diploma work, a one-act opera-oratorio, *Earth and Heaven*, after Byron; immediately after graduation started teaching in the Gnessin School of Music in Moscow; produced, in rapid succession, several collections of songs, the second and third concertos, pieces for pianoforte, and the second symphony dedicated to Sergei Kussevitsky; 1905–07 studied conducting in Berlin with Oscar Fried, and in 1908, back in Russia, made his first public appearance as a conductor, in which capacity he is still prominent; 1910 published his third symphony, "Ilya Muromets"; 1913 moved to Kiev and took charge of the composition class in the conservatoire, of which he was elected Director in the following year; since 1920 has lived in Moscow where he has taken an active part in creative, educational and social work; has undertaken concert tours and travels connected with the study of folklore; written many compositions based upon the national musical cultures of Russia, Ukraine, Azerbaijan, Uzbekistan and other republics; during the first years of Revolution was at the head of the Musical Section of the Moscow Department of People's Education, directed the organization of concerts in workers' clubs, and gradually acquired the authority of both an eminent composer and an able organizer; 1926–7 wrote his ballet *The Red Poppy*; 1923 undertook a detailed

9

study of the Azerbaijan folklore and national music, as a result of which he wrote his opera, *Shah Senem*, completed in 1925 and re-arranged in 1933/4; after a similar research in the Uzbek folklore, wrote in 1936 his musical drama *Hulsara*; later worked on Ukrainian songs which were familiar to him since childhood and by 1939 completed the symphonic poem "To the memory of a great people's poet" dedicated to Taras Shevchenko on the occasion of 125th anniversary of his birth; 1937 elected chairman of the Management Committee of the Moscow Union of Composers; 1939 chairman of the Organizing Committee of the Union of Soviet Composers, at the head of which he remains to this day; 1937 was awarded the Order of the Red Banner; 1938 the Order of Merit; as far back as 1925 awarded the title of Merited Artist of R.S.F.S.R.; later governments of various republics bestowed on him titles in appreciation of his work in the field of national music, and in 1938 the Government of the U.S.S.R. conferred upon him the high title of People's Artist of the U.S.S.R.; received in the following year the degree of Doctor of Sciences (research in art).

During the war he has written remarkable patriotic works: overture "For the Happiness of the Fatherland", songs, marches and the opera *Rachel* on the subject of Guy de Maupassant's story, *Mademoiselle Fifi*, depicting the French people's hatred of the German invaders during the Franco-Prussian war of 1870–1.

In his development he is organically related to the 5 on the one side and Chaikovsky and Taneev on the other; he absorbed the best traditions of Russian music and handed them on to his many brilliant pupils among whom are to be included Sergei Prokofiev, Nicolas Myaskovsky, and Aram Khachaturian.

MICHAEL F. GNESSIN

★

B. 1883 in Rostov-on-Don; studied composition for seven years in the St. Petersburg Conservatoire under Rimsky-Korsakov and Lyadov, graduating in 1908; 1911 went to German where he stayed for three years; 1914 returned to Russia and again went to live in Rostov-on-Don where he stayed for seven years; made a tour in Western Europe and Palestine, and on returning in 1923, settled in Moscow; 1936 appointed professor of the Leningrad Conservatory.

He derives inspiration from Jewish national music. In his symphonic, chamber and vocal works he draws on Arab-Semitic songs and their luxurious ornamentation, preserving at the same time a strong bond with the Russian musical culture.

MICHAEL M. IPPOLITOV-IVANOV

★

B. 1859 in Gatchina, near St. Petersburg, son of a fitter employed in a casting workshop; as a child was taught to sing, first at home and later in the elementary school; at eight started to learn violin, and at ten went to live in St. Petersburg where his musical training was carried on in the various classes attached to the choir of the Isaaky Cathedral (1872–5) and in the St. Peterburg Conservatoire (1875–82); there studied composition with Rimsky-Korsakov and learned to play the double-bass and to conduct; during last three years in the conservatoire met Balakirev, Borodin and Mussorgsky; after graduating from the conservatoire in 1882 settled in Tiflis; composed a great deal and engaged in educational activities which played an important role in the development of musical culture in the Caucasus; as conductor performed an extensive repertoire comprising classical and modern works; directed the local musical school which was subsequently re-organized into a conservatoire; collected, studied and arranged rich ethnographical material, some of which was used later on by himself as well as by other composers, particularly by Chaikovsky. National principles in art, so well developed by Russian masters, made a lasting impression on his pupils—especially on the leading Georgian composer Zahkari Paliashvili and his followers.

In 1893 he and his wife, the singer, Barbasa Zarudina, were appointed professors in the Moscow Conservatoire, where he lectured on history of music and theory of composition. His many eminent pupils included Glier, Vassilyenko, Igumnov, Nikolayev. In 1894 he completed his symphonic suite "Caucasian Sketches". This work, in which are introduced themes of Georgian and Armenian folklore, was followed by the "Armenian Rhapsody" for symphonic orchestra and the second suite "Iveria", written on themes of Georgian popular songs. In 1900

12

his opera *Assya* (after Turgeniev's story) was performed for the first time. In 1905 he was appointed director of the Moscow Conservatoire and held this post until 1922 when for reasons of health he had to give up the administrative work but continued to hold his professorship. At the end of 1910 his new opera, *Treachery*, was produced for the first time, and in November, 1916, the Bolshoi Theatre presented the opera, *Olé from Nordland*, after the story of M. Iersen describing the life of Norwegian peasantry.

After the October Revolution he indefatiguably carried on his creative, teaching and social activities; 1922 was elected chairman of the All-Union Association of Writers and Composers, and in the same year was awarded the title of People s Artist of the Republic; 1924–5 was director and professor of the Tiflis Conservatoire, and when back in Moscow in 1925, despite his advanced age, started to work in the Bolshoi Theatre in the capacity of art director and conductor.

In the years following the October Revolution he wrote a number of symphonic poems, four suites for orchestra, 'Voroshilov's march" for orchestra, opera *The Last Barricade*, three acts of the opera *Wedding* (the first act was written by Mussorgski, after the story of Gogol), and a great many other works of various types. Early in 1934 the jubilee of his fifty years' musical activity was celebrated all over the Union, and he was presented with the Order of the Red Banner. Until the very last days of his life, he was full of energy and will to work, but he was unable to carry all his plans into effect; thus he left unfinished the scores of his second symphony, "Karelia", for symphonic and wind orchestra with choir, a children's opera after a Caucasian story, and other works.

He passed away in the night of 28th January, 1935.

DMITRI B. KABALEVSKY

★

B. 1904 in St. Petersburg, son of a civil servant; at six played
the piano by ear, but did not start to study music systematically
until 1918, when his family came to live in Moscow; entered the,
Skriabin Musical School, and completed his course in piano in
1925, studying composition at the same time with Vassilyenko
and Katuar; on leaving this school was admitted into the Moscow
Conservatoire where he pursued his studies under Goldenweiser
and at the same time taught the piano in the Skriabin School;
continued to work with Katuar at the conservatoire, but these
studies were interrupted in 1926 by the death of this outstanding
teacher; then joined the composition class of the composer and
teacher Nicolas Myaskovsky; completed studies in composition
in 1929, and in piano in 1930; on graduating from the conservatoire his name was engraved on the "golden panel"; started to
teach soon after leaving the Conservatoire and continues this work
in the capacity of professor of composition in the Moscow
Conservatoire.

He has produced a series of musical works in all genres: opera,
ballet, symphonic, vocal, chamber music, theatre and film music,
popular song; he has also devoted much time to work as music
critic and has published numerous articles and research studies
on music; he is editor of the review *Soviet Music*; in 1939 he was
elected member of the Presidium of the Organizing Committee
of the Union of Soviet Composers, and in 1940 was awarded the
Order of Merit.

In the first months of war he published numerous war songs, a
long cantata for choir, soloists and orchestra "Our Great Fatherland", and—a little later—the suite "People's Avengers" for
choir and symphonic orchestra to the words of the young poet,
Eugene Dolmatovsky, written both by the poet and the composer during their sojourn at the front.

On the occasion of the twenty-fifth anniversary of the October Revolution he wrote a new opera. While his first opera, *Cola Brugnon*, after Romain Rolland, transports us into France of the period of the Renaissance, the second—*Before Moscow*—is related to the events which took place in the autumn of 1941 on the approaches to Moscow.

The most profound influences to which he was subjected and which determined his artistic formation were those of Mussorgsky, Borodin, Chaikovsky, and, partly, Skriabin. A close relation to folk song manifested itself already in his early works—the string quartet and the first concerto for pianoforte—where he developed themes of popular songs recorded by himself. In the ballet "The Golden Spikes" the affinity with national Byelorussian folklore is clearly discernable, whilst the suite "People's Avengers", written at the South-Western front, shows the influence of Ukrainian popular music.

GRIGORI V. KILADZE

★

B. 1905 in the town of Batum; began to study music at an
early age and benefited greatly from his participation in the school
choir, under the direction of the leading Georgian composer
Zakhari Paliashvili; on leaving school worked as a greaser in the
electric power station, then as a hand in automobile workshops and
as a film mechanic, devoting every free minute to music; composed,
played the violin and conducted the orchestra of the Association
of Young Georgian Musicians; 1925 entered the Tiflis Conservatoire where he worked under the well-known Georgian musician,
professor Dmitri Arakishvili; later studied in the Leningrad Conservatoire under Ryazanov and Shcherbachev; after graduating
from the Conservatoire taught in the Tiflis Conservatoire, and
for a number of years directed the musical section of the Georgian
dramatic theatre named after Shota Rustavelli; led the Union of
Georgian Soviet composers and the Tiflis Conservatoire.

In 1936 his symphonic poem "Gandeghilly" (The Hermit),
written to the text of the well-known Georgian writer Ilya Chav-
chavadze was performed for the first time. Its subject is the
victory of humanism over the morbid survivals of the Middle
Ages. Following this work, which in 1941 won a Stalin prize,
he wrote a symphony, and shortly before the war completed an
opera about Lado Ketskhovelli, a Georgian bolshevik and a com-
panion of Stalin.

His music is organically derived from Georgian folklore and
bears the melodic character of Georgian popular music.

He has been presented with the Order of Merit.

16

ARAM I. KHACHATURIAN

★

B. 1904 in Tiflis, son of a poor artisan, who until the revolution had no means of providing him with an adequate education; 1923 came to Moscow and entered the Gnessin School of Music, where he studied violoncello playing; after two years was admitted into the course personally directed by Gnessin; on finishing the school in 1926 entered the Moscow Conservatoire, where he continued to study under Gnessin, attending at the same time the classes of Vassilenko and Litinskov; it was Miaskovsky, however, who became his principal teacher; 1934 graduated from the Conservatoire, his name being engraved on the Golden Panel of Honour.

At that time he was already the author of numerous compositions, among them a trio for clarinet, violin, and piano, sonatas for violin and piano, Dance Suite for orchestra, and finally the "First Symphony", which was his diploma work at the Conservatoire. This was soon followed by a piano concerto, by the "Poem to Stalin" for orchestra and chorus, by the ballet "Happiness" (which he is now revising) and by a violin concerto. To these works must be added the music which he wrote to many productions of the Moscow Arts Theatre (Kremlevski curanti) of the Eugen Vakhtangov Theatre (Mascarade) and of the Armenian State Theatre (Macbeth), as well as to several films, such as "Pepo", the theme song of which has become one of Armenia's national songs.

His music is deeply rooted in the folklore of his native Armenia, but in addition he draws from the sources of Georgian, Russian, Ukrainian, Turkish, Turkmenian, and Irano-azerbaijan national melodies. At the same time, his work reveals marked features common to West-European art forms.

In 1939 he was awarded the Order of Lenin, and in the following year won the Stalin prize for his violin concerto. For the twenty-fifth anniversary he is writing his 2nd symphony, and has composed a series of patriotic songs for the Red Army.

17

TIKHON N. KHRENNIKOV

★

B. 1913, received his initial musical training at home; in addition to playing the piano, attempted to compose music at an early age; serious musical studies began at the Gnessin School of Music in Moscow (1929–32) and continued at the Moscow Conservatoire; 1936 graduated, his name being engraved in the Golden Panel of Merit of the Conservatoire. Vissarion Shebalin was his principal teacher.

His first compositions—a concerto for piano and orchestra, songs and piano pieces, as well as the 1st Symphony, written in 1935, are all influenced by the Soviet composers Prokoviev, Shostakovitch, and Shebalin. These influences, however, have not only determined his creative work, they have also led him to further research. The sources of folklore, to which Khrenikov often turned, e.g. in his opera *In the Storm* on the subject of N. Wirt's novel *Loneliness*, proved very beneficial to his work.

In 1942 he won the Stalin prize for his music to the film "The Pigs and the Shepherd".

In one year of war, he has written a number of patriotic songs, a musical comedy and has begun working on a ballet.

GLIER

PROKOFIEV

MOSSOLOV

SHOSTAKOVITCH

DZERZHINSKY   KHACHATURIAN
        MIASKOVSKY   KHRENNIKOV

VICTOR S. KOSSENKO

★

B. 1896 in Petersburg, at the age of eight given piano lessons by his pianist sister—a student at the Warsaw Conservatoire; later became a pupil of Professor Mikhailovsky; when twelve years old wrote his first cycle of pieces for the piano, which were followed by other vocal and instrumental compositions; 1914 completed his secondary education and entered the St. Petersburg Conservatoire to study piano playing under Irene Mikhlashevsky and the theory of composition under Nikolai Sokolov and Maximilian Steinberg; graduated in 1918, and went to live in the Ukraine, where his activities as a composer, pianist, and teacher reached their height.

At first he spent a few years in Zhitomir, writing several sonatas for piano, poems, nocturnes, études, chamber music compositions, songs, etc. His arrival brought in its wake a noticeable revival of the musical life in the city. He often appeared on concert platforms, and taught in the School of Music which, on his death, was named after him. From Zhitomir he frequently travelled to Moscow, Kiev, Kharkov and other towns of the Soviet Union, fulfilling numerous concert engagements as a composer and pianist. In 1929 he moved to Kiev and was appointed professor of pianoforte and theory of composition at the Conservatoire. He continued, however, his public appearances at concerts, as well as his creative work. During this period he wrote the "Heroic Overture" to the fifteenth anniversary of the October Revolution—"Moldav Poem" for orchestra—Concerto for piano and orchestra—a cycle of pieces for piano—ballads, —choruses—arrangements of Ukrainian folksongs, etc. Shortly before his death, he began working on the opera *Marina* on the theme of the poem by the Ukrainian poet Taras Shevchenko. In 1938 he was awarded to Order of the Red Workers' Banner. A grave illness, which confined him to his bed for many months, became gradually worse, and he passed away on 3rd October, 1938.

After his death, his friends, Boris Liatoshinsky and Lev Revutzin, performed the task of preparing for publication the manuscript compositions which had not appeared in his lifetime.

His work reveals a strong influence of Chaikovsky, Rachmaninov and West-European romantic music, in particular of Chopin and Schumann, and has derived great benefit from the introduction and adaptation of themes from the melodious treasures of Ukrainian and Moldavian folksongs.

LEV. K. KNIPPER

★

B. in 1898 in Tiflis; taught himself to play the piano when still a child, with the sole aid of a musical handbook, and at the age of fifteen or sixteen began to compose small pieces for piano; returning from the Far East after five years' service in the Army, entered the Gnessin School of Music in Moscow, where he studied under Glier, Helas Gnessin and Dimitri Rogal-Levitzkov.

His Symphonic Poem, Op. 1, "The Legend of a Plaster God", written in 1924, was perfcrmed by the Philadelphia Symphony Orchestra, conducted by Leopold Stokovsky. This work was followed by two symphonies, the opera-ballet *Candide*, completed in 1927, the opera *Northern Wind* (1930), and other compositions, in which the influence of the French impressionists is seen to recede gradually, in favour of the influence of Stravinsky and, to some extent, of West-European expressionism.

In 1931 he completed his research into the folklore of the mountainous regions of Tadjskistan. He wrote down over 150 songs, which were subsequently utilized in compositions such as the Symphonic Suite "Vantch", the Overture "Vakhio Bolo", etc.

In the following year he worked as a musical instructor in various units of the Red Army and Navy, acquainting himself with the life of the Soviet soldiers, to whom he dedicated his Third Symphony—"To the Far Eastern Army"—and his Fifth Symphony—"Poem of the Komsomol Fighter". Mass battle songs are introduced into these symphonies.

Following this he wrote the song "Cavalry of the Steppes".

Since the outbreak of war, Lev Knipper has written a number of new battle songs, his Eighth Symphony and a Violin Concerto

MARIAN V. KOVAL

*

B. 1907 in the hamlet Pristan-Voznessey, near the northern town of Olonezka, son of an agricultural estate-manager; usually) spent the summer at his uncle's in Nijni-Novgorod (now Gorky) and in the winter lived in St. Petersburg, where from the age of five he received piano lessons at the School of Music; continued these studies from 1918 to 1921 in Nijni, and then again at the St. Petersburg School of Music; 1925 began to study composition; at the end of the same year was admitted to the Moscow Conservatoire, working under Gnessin until 1930; subsequently worked for a few years privately under Miaskovsky, and to this latter period belongs his unfinished opera *Graf Nulin* after Alexander Pushkin.

In the course of a few years he has written an enormous number of songs and choral compositions, mostly collected in cycles; he is drawn to the treasures of Russian poetry, which pervades his cycle of ballads to verses by Pushkin and Nekrassov; he is stirred by the past of his people (cycles "The Accursed Past"—"1905"—"Tale of the Partisans") and full of love for its leaders (two cycles of songs to Lenin—cycle of songs to Stalin). He is equally inspired by West-European and American poetry, as is shown in the cycle of "Songs of Loneliness" to verses by Spanish poets.

In 1939 he completed his Oratorio for solo chorus and orchestra, "Emelian Pugachev" (after the text of Vassili Kamensky). In the same year he wrote the delightful children's opera "The Wolf and the Seven Goats" (on the theme of the popular nursery tale), and then began to work on the opera *Emelian Pugachev*, in which he frequently made use of the material of his Oratorio. This opera was not completed until 1942, because the outbreak of the German-Soviet war was felt by him to be a call to express in his music the determination and will to victory of the whole

22

Russian people. Thus were born many battle songs, and the Oratorio "The People's Sacred War".

At present he is putting the finishing touches to his new Oratorio "Valery Chkalov", dedicated to the memory of the great contemporary aviator.

His music is profoundly national and firmly rooted in the traditions of the Russian classics and of Mussorgsky in particular; it is permeated with the kindred spirit of Russian folklore with its melodiousness and power of expression, which are within the grasp of the entire people.

ALEXANDER A. KREIN

★

B. 1883 in Nijni-Novgorod (now Gorki) into a musical family; his father was a fine violin player and a collector of folksongs; his elder brother David, a violinist and the leader of the Orchestra of the Moscow "Bolshoi Theatre", his brother Gregori and nephew Juilan are also composers; began to study music early, and made attempts in composition already at the age of seven; entered the Moscow Conservatoire in 1897, from which he graduated as violoncellist in 1908, having studied under Prof. A. Glen; at the same time devoted great attention to creative work and to the study of the theory of music; on leaving the Conservatoire spent a further year at the Moscow Philharmonic College to pursue this study.

His creative work embraces a variety of genres of musical art, from the opera and symphony to piano and vocal compositions. Already in his first major work, the symphonic poem "Solomon", he reveals his attraction to the ornamental Arab-Semitic style and to themes from biblical sources. In both the First Symphony and the Sonata for piano, the century old "Song of Songs" is made use of.

Turning to the ancient and forgotten sources of human musical culture, he revived them and gave them a prominent place in his compositions. Orientalism is only one of the elements in Krein's music, but this element is organically linked with the Spanish-Moorish motives which determine the character of his first ballet "Laurencia", on the subject of Fuente Ovehuna. A different effect is obtained in the second ballet, completed only a short time ago, "The Rape of Tatania", which is dedicated to recent events. The music of this ballet is closely related to the style of Russian national music.

24

BORIS N. LIATOSHINSKY

★

B. 1895, in the Ukrainian town of Zhitomir, son of a teacher of history; as a child had lessons in violin and piano and made his first attempts in composition; wrote songs and chamber music, which were performed by local musicians; 1913 he began to study in Kiev under Glier, whose course at the Conservatoire he completed in 1918, graduating also in the same year from the Law faculty of the Kiev University; wrote a number of compositions when still a student at the Conservatoire, including a String Quartet, First Symphony (which was his diploma work) and others; on completing his course of study at the Conservatoire, wrote within a short space of time two further String Quartets, a Trio for Pianoforte, several Sonatas, a cycle of piano pieces "Reflection", and many songs; in 1927, at the Musical Contest of the Soviet Republics on the occasion of the tenth anniversary of the October Revolution, won the first prize for his Overture on Four Ukrainian Popular Themes; in 1929 completed his first opera, *The Golden Hoop*, about the heroic struggle of the Ukrainian people against the Mongolians in the thirteenth century, and in 1937 composed his second opera, *Schors*, about Commander Nicolai Schors, one of the heroes of the Civil War in 1918; in subsequent years composed the tripartite Second Symphony, Cantata Zapovit (to words by the great Ukrainian poet Taras Shevchenko), Solemn Cantata for Solo, Chorus and Orchestra (on the occasion of the sixtieth anniversary of Joseph Stalin) and several cycles of ballads.

His early works reflect the influence of Russian classical music, in particular of Borodine, and to some extent of Scriabin, Wagner and Liszt. In his later compositions there are also traces of the influence of French impressionism and of West-European expressionism.

His activity as a teacher, which began in 1920, has been continuous to this day. As a professor at the Kiev and Moscow Conservatoires he has been responsible for the training of several generations of Soviet composers. At the same time, he has played a leading role in the work of the Union of Soviet Composers, in his capacity as member of the Presidium of its Organizing Committee, and as Chairman of the Ukrainian Union of Composers since 1939.

In 1938 the Soviet Government conferred upon him the Order of Merit.

In the course of the war, he has written several dozen vocal compositions, a suite for pianoforte "1941", and has started to work on his Third Symphony for the twenty-fifth anniversary of the October Revolution.

KONSTANTIN Y. LISTOV

★

B. 1900 of working-class origin; as a child played the mandoline, balalaika and the piano by ear, and in 1914 entered a school
for music in Tsaritsin—now Stalingrad; he graduated in 1917,
having completed courses in pianoforte and the theory of composition; enrolled voluntarily in the following year in the ranks of
the Red Army, and was frequently in action; was seriously
wounded at the time of the heroic defence of Tsaritsin.

The soldiers of the Tenth Army, to which he belonged, often
sang songs composed by him at the front. The command of the
Army, having noticed his talent, decided to send him to Saratov to
continue his musical education. There he spent three years, 1919
to 1921, and graduated from the Conservatoire after studying
composition under Professor Rudolph, a pupil of Sergei Taneev.
But even during these years he often went to the front and visited
units of the Red Army and Navy, teaching the men the songs
which he had written. From the atmosphere of the front line he
derived inspiration for new songs. In 1923 he moved to Moscow,
where he is still living, engaged in creative work. In the course
of his years of study at the Conservatoire, he wrote several symphonic compositions, and a Concerto for piano and orchestra.
On his arrival in Moscow he devoted much time to a number of
musical comedies, among them *The Queen is Wrong*, *The Ice
House* and *Jenny*, which were successfully produced in several
theatres. In addition, he wrote the music for the production of
the *Bourgeois Gentil'homme*, by Molière, *Money Box*, by Lyabitch,
and for satirical revues produced in Moscow's "Little Theatre".

His main field remains, however, the song of battle. He is
thoroughly acquainted with the life of the Red Army and Navy,
with the moods and aspirations of the men, with whom he fought
shoulder to shoulder during the years of the Civil War. This is
why his songs are so popular in the Red Army and Navy, and

27

among the whole Soviet people—for example, the famous "Song of Tachanka", "Beloved Grass", "On Guard", "In the Dug-out", etc. In all, he has written over two hundred songs, many of them composed in the course of the war.

NINA V. MAKAROVA

★

B. 1908 in the hamlet of Yurin, situated on the left bank of the Volga, daughter of a village teacher; showed from early childhood a passionate love for music, and keen interest in the Russian and Mari folksongs; at fifteen began to study at the School of Music in Gorky, and in 1927 went to Moscow where her training continued under Nicolai Miaskovsky; graduated in 1935 from the Conservatoire.

She is attracted by both instrumental and vocal music—ballads and choruses appear alongside a sonatina and six etudes for piano, pieces for oboe, and finally a tripartite First Symphony, the latter being the composer's diploma work, performed for the first time in Moscow in 1938.

In 1938 she wrote a series of settings to the verses of the Georgian poet Shota Rustaveli, the author of "Knights in Tiger Skins". In 1940 she began working on the opera *Courage*, dedicated to the young builders of the Soviet far-eastern town Komsmolsk. Her songs, in particular the children's song about Stalin were already popular prior to the war. She is now writing music with added intensity. Continuing her work on the opera, she has composed several patriotic songs—"The Sea Song", "The Ural Song", "The Polar Song".

NICOLAI I. MIASKOVSKY

★

B. 1881 in the Fortress of Novo Georgiensk, near Warsaw, son of a military engineer, professor at the Military Academy; from Novo Georgiensk his family moved to the distant Orenburg, thence to Kazan, and finally to Nijni Novgorod—now Gorki— where he joined the Cadet Corps, but assiduously continued to study music; pursued his studies in St. Petersburg and in 1895 on graduating from the Cadet Corps entered the College for Military Engineering and completed the appointed course in three years; was then posted to the Sappers Battalion, first in Moscow and later in St. Petersburg, and only in 1907 succeeded in resigning his commission so as to devote himself wholeheartedly to his art.

His first attempts in composition—a large collection of pianoforte preludes—were made as early as 1896; he took private lessons in composition from Glier and I. Kryjanovsky, and finally in 1906 entered the St. Petersburg Conservatoire, where he studied under Rimsky-Korsakov, Anatole Liadov, and Josef Vitol. In the first year it was difficult to reconcile his military service with attendance at the Conservatoire, but on his release from the Army in the following year he became extremely prolific. In 1907–8 he wrote four sonatas and several dozen pieces for pianoforte, a string quartet, and finally his first symphony, which earned him the approval of Glasunov. Then followed the synfonic poem "Silence", an overture and a synfonietta. In the spring of 1911 he completed the Conservatoire's course of study in composition under Liadov; among his contemporaries at the Conservatoire were Prokovev, Assafiev, Saminsky, and others. In the period between his graduation and the outbreak of the first world war, he wrote two more sonatas, the symphonic poem "Alastor" (on words by Shelley) and a number of vocal and piano compositions; his works began to be performed and to

30

appear in print; he spent the years 1914–17 on the Austrian front, where he was seriously wounded, and after the October Revolution until 1921 he worked on the General Staff in Moscow; in 1918–19 he wrote two symphonies, one of which is his Fifth Symphony, performed for the first time in Moscow in 1920.

Since 1921 he has held the post of Professor at the Moscow Conservatoire; his pupils have included Aram Khachaturian, Vissarion Shebalin, Leonid Polovinkin, Vano Muradeli, Michael Starokadomsky, Victor Bely, Dimitry Kabalevsky, and others. He serves his pupils as an example of talent, skill, and perseverance. Every year he composes new works; among the best known are the Sixth Symphony, completed in 1923—the Eighth Symphony (1925) associated with the figure of the popular hero Stepan Rasin, the Tenth Symphony, inspired by Pushkin's poem "The Slow Horseman", the Twelfth "Kolkhoz" Symphony, the Sixteenth Symphony with the Funeral March composed after the disaster of the aeroplane "Maxime Gorky", and the 21st Symphony, which won the award of the Stalin Prize in 1941. Other symphonic compositions appeared at the same time, a concerto for violin, chamber music, etc. In 1941–2, in the days of the war, he wrote the 22nd Symphonic Ballad and the 23rd Symphonic Suite on Kabardino-Balkarsk themes, the Seventh String Quartet and a series of patriotic songs.

His creative work is closely related to the general trend of development of Russian classical symphonic music, and reveals the influence of Mussorgsky, Borodin, and Taneev, with their leanings towards the popular melody and the Russian folksong.

A genuine aspiration towards simplicity and sincerity marks every step in his long creative development.

ALEXANDER VASSILEVICH MOSSOLOV

★

B. 1900 in Kiev, son of an artist and singer; 1904 his family
moved to Moscow; 1921, on completing his secondary education,
took a course in composition under Glier at the Moscow Conservatoire, graduating in 1925, having at the same time studied
pianoforte playing under Gregory Prokovev; wrote whilst still
at the Conservatoire a symphonic poem "Twilight", five sonatas
for pianoforte, a cycle of settings of verses by Nikolai Guimiliev
and Alexander Blok; his diploma work was a cantata for choir,
solo, and orchestra "Sphynx" on the test of Oscar Wilde's
poem.

All these early composition bear evidence of his modern
tendencies, of his creative affinity to Prokovev, Steinberg, and
Hindemith; their influence is also apparent in many of his later
works—in three symphonies, two concertos for pianoforte, a
string quartet, and in particular in the symphonic episode "The
Iron Foundry" composed after leaving the Conservatoire.

To his creative work should be added his work as a virtuoso,
since he frequently fulfilled concert engagements as a pianist. In
1927-8, he became the Acting (Responsible) Secretary of the
Russian Section of the International Association of Contemporary Music, which was then joined by many representative
Soviet composers. In subsequent years he travelled in Central
Asia, devoting his time to the study of the folklore of Khirghizia,
Turkmenia, and Tadjikistan. As a result of this research, he
produced several new compositions among them "Khirghiz
rhapsody" for mezzo-soprano, chorus, and orchestra, "Turk-
menian-overture" for orchestra, a cycle "Turkmenian Nights"
for pianoforte. These compositions mark a turning point in
Mossolov's style, which has further matured in the works of the
following period—the Concerto for Harp and Orchestra, and
the Fourth Symphony—completed in 1941, which is dedicated

to the memory of Lermontov on the 100th anniversary of his death. Since the commencement of the war, he has written a one-act opera *Signal*, and a series of patriotic songs and choruses.

I. MURADELI

★

B. 1908, of peasant origin, in the Georgian hamlet of Gory, the birthplace of Joseph Stalin.

From early childhood he listened to the songs of his people, memorized them, playing them on the mandoline, the guitar or the lute. At the age of eleven he began to compose songs in the Georgian language and to sing them, imitating the style of folksongs. On leaving school in Gory, he entered the school of music in Tiflis to study singing.

In 1926 he was admitted without an examination into the Tiflis Conservatoire, where he studied under S. Barkhidarian, V. Shtcherbatchev, and the Georgian composer and historian, D. Arkishvil. He graduated from the Conservatoire in 1931, and spent the three following years in Tiflis, where he wrote a considerable amount of theatre music. He was the leader of the musical section of the Young Workers' Theatre and promoted many new vocal productions. In 1934 he came to Moscow, was admitted into the second year of the Conservatoire, and completed his musical training in 1938, under Schechter and Miaskovsky. For his Diploma work he wrote the two first movements of his Symphony in Four Movements, dedicated to the memory of S. Kirov, finishing it in the following year. In 1939 he wrote his First Cantata to Stalin, which was followed almost immediately by the second Cantata, and then by "Zdravitza" for chorus and orchestra, dedicated to the Soviet people and the Fatherland.

Throughout this period he was actively engaged in the writing of film and theatre music for the productions at the Chamber Theatre, the Moscow Dramatic Theatre and others. Since the outbreak of war he has composed the music to the films "Retribution" and "Hatred", over twenty patriotic songs and ballads, among them the ballad "Father and Son" for bass and orchestra, and the popular song "Dovator's Men", dedicated to the heroic

KOVAL LISTOV

KREIN KOSSENKO

SHTCHERBATCHEV

DUNAYEVSKY

POLOVINKIN

VASSILYENKO

exploits of General Dovator's cavalry regiments. In the summer of 1942 the composer began working on his second symphony "The War of Liberation".

His music is deeply rooted in the Georgian folklore. Yet he never has recourse to direct quotations from popular song. The melodious structure of Georgian national music and its marked diatonic character are at the source of his style, but its themes are interwoven into his compositions which remain original, although unmistakably Georgian in spirit.

Whilst still a student, he was elected in 1937 as President of the Youth Section of the Association of Soviet Composers. In 1938 he became the Secretary of the Association and in 1939 a member of its Organizing Committee and the chairman of the Musical Fund of the U.S.S.R.

Since the outbreak of war he joined the Anti-Fascist Youth Committee and has frequently visited the front.

ANDREI F. PASHTCHENKO

★

B. 1883 in Rostov-on-Don; received his initial musical training at home, and although his first compositions date back to his early youth, his choice of a profession was not made until 1914; entered the St. Petersburg Conservatoire in that year, where for three years studied the theory of composition under Maximilian Steinberg and Joseph Vitol; after graduating from the Conservatoire, engaged in teaching and social musical activity, but devoted most of his time to creative work; prolific in almost every genre, but particularly in the field of oratorio-operatic, symphonic and choral music.

His compositions bear signs of the influence of Wagner and Scriabin. At the same time, he was deeply engrossed in the study of folk-lore, in particular of Russian folksongs; this is apparent in his choral music, in his arrangements of popular songs and in his symphonies, particularly in his Sixth and Seventh Symphonies, "The Triumphant" and "The Pioneer", his "Red Fleet Overture", etc.

Gradually, his music has drawn increasingly from the source of folklore, and falls into line with the main trend of development of Russian classical music. The earlier tendencies are supplanted by the influence of Mussorgsky and Borodin, which asserts itself in the composer's operas—in the tragic *The Revolt of the Eagle*, in the farcial *Tsar Maximilian* (based on a popular story) and in *Pompadours* (on the text of Michael Saltikov-Shtchedrin).

Only recently he showed his courage and valiance by remaining in Leningrad throughout the siege of the city, never interrupting for a single day his creative work.

His "Requiem in memory of the Heroes who have laid down their lives in the great War of Liberation", completed in 1942, was written for orchestra and chorus, to the composer's own words, in praise of the gallant deeds of the Russian soldiers.

36

Then in the midst of the appalling destruction wrought by Hitler's barbarians, he composed his "Festive Overture", which will resound with its full vigour in the not distant days of the enemy's defeat.

DIMITRI I. POKRASS

*

B. 1899 in Kiev, son of a cattle driver, revealed musical talent in early childhood; his brothers worked as cinema musicians, the older ones sharing their experience with the younger.

But coincidence alone assisted this son of a poor family to gain a musical education. In 1914 M. Guelever, the Principal of the St. Petersburg Conservatoire heard him play and took him there to attend his classes; he spent three years in the St. Petersburg Conservatoire, earning his living by playing the piano in cinemas and restaurants and learning to compose variety songs.

In 1917 he returned to his native Kiev, and in 1919 enrolled as a volunteer in the Red Army, where he fought in the ranks of the First Cavalry Division and dedicated many songs to its glorious advance, among them the "Budenny March". These songs attracted the attention of the Soviet High Command. In 1921 he was introduced to Marshal Voroshilov, who advised him to go to Moscow. In Moscow, where the composer has been living to date, his creative work unfolded. He wrote music for theatrical productions, revues, and songs, and appeared on the platform as a conductor and pianist. For ten years, from 1926 to 1936, he was in charge of the musical section of the Moscow "Music Hall", and subsequently assumed the art direction of the Jazz Ensemble in the Railway Workers' House of Culture. He wrote the music to many Soviet films, among them "The Doctors of the Tropics", "Worker and Peasant", "The 20th May", "Son of the Working People", "A Thought about Cossack Golot", "If War breaks out to-morrow . . .", "A young Lady with Character", "Field, my little Field", "Tank Crew", "In Defence of the Fatherland", etc. For his work in film music he was awarded the Stalin Prize in 1941. Most of his songs were composed in collaboration with his brother Daniel Pokrass.

Since the outbreak of war the Pokrass brothers have composed many new patriotic songs, which on many occasions were written at the front. In 1938 the Soviet Government bestowed upon Dimitri Pokrass the Order of the Workers' Red Banner

LEONID A. POLOVINKIN

★

B. 1894, son of a railway engineer, in the small Siberian town Kurgan. When two years old, his whole family moved to Moscow; was educated in the capital first in a secondary school, and in 1917 entered the Law Faculty of the Moscow University; was keenly interested in literature, history, and philosophy, and his command of a number of languages enabled him to read the classics in their originals. His greatest interest was music; he did not enter the Conservatoire, however, until 1915; there he studied piano playing under Prof. Lev Konyus and, after the latter's departure from Moscow, under Prof. Kippa. At the same time he took lessons in the theory of composition. He studied fugue under Glier, while Sergei Vassilyenko taught him musical form and Georgy Katiara free composition. He graduated from the Conservatoire in 1924, and his name was engraved in the Conservatoire's golden panel. For some time after he left the Conservatoire he engaged in teaching, taking charge of a course of form analysis. In collaboration with Dimitri Kabalevski, he prepared for publication the *Handbook of Musical Forms*, written by his late master, Georgi Katiara.

But essentially his life has been devoted to creative work, which is amazingly varied as regards contents as well as genres. He has written operas, ballets, and symphonic compositions as well as theatre and pianoforte music. His first opera is written to Pushkin's delightful story, *A Tale of the Fisherman and the Fish*, and is deeply rooted in Russian popular art and folklore. The second opera transports one into another country and a world of completely different images; it is the opera *Hero*, written to the text of John M. Synge's three-act comedy *The Playboy of the Western World*, wherein one can hear the themes and style of Irish folksongs. His use of folklore, however, is always conditioned by the particular requirements of his subject, and does not constitute a distinctive feature of his compositions.

His music is drawn towards West-European harmony. It is possible to detect traces of Skriabin's and Brahms' influence in the first symphonic sonata, whilst the miniatures for pianoforte reveal certain features in common with Sergei Prokoviev's music.

His great interest in jazz music is worth noting. The orchestral style of jazz was used by him in film music (in particular in the film "Marionettes", with his popular "Song of Paraguay"). Shortly before the war he completed a Jazz Concerto for solo instruments and orchestra.

Simultaneously with eccentric compositions and dances for pianoforte, with romantic symphonies and sonatas, he produced four monumental "Telescopes" for large orchestra.

Since the war, however, he became engrossed in one problem only—the defeat and destruction of the enemy. To this aim he dedicated many patriotic songs, written in 1941–2, the Heroic Overture, and the Sixth Symphony, on which he is working at present.

GAVRIEL N. POPOV

★

B. 1904 in Novocherkass, son of a professor of languages, the high cultural level of the family was reflected in the encyclopaedic education he received. From childhood he had a command of the principal foreign languages and was well read in universal literature, history, and philosophy. After having gone through the School of Music at Rostov-on-Don, where he studied piano playing under Prof. V. Shaube, he moved to St. Petersburg, and entered the Conservatoire in 1922. He graduated in 1930 having completed the pianoforte course under Leonid Nikolaieff and the course in theory of composition under Maximilian Steinberg and Vladimir Shtcherbatchev.

Already in his early works—such as the "Suite Major" and "Expressions and Melodies" for pianoforte, the Sextet and the "First Symphony", which was awarded the first prize in the All Union competition for the best symphonic composition—the individual traits of his music find their expression. His motto is: "Art must be contemporary."

His creative quest is, therefore, dictated by life itself. This is felt forcibly in his film music—in the films "Chapaiev", "Komsomol leads Electrification", "The New Fatherland", etc.

When composing on themes from the past, he views them with the eyes of a modern artist, and not of an ethnograph or historian, as is apparent in his first opera *The Slow Horseman* to Pushkin's famous poem, in the "Heroic Intermesso", written since the war, for chorus, solo, and orchestra, and finally in the opera *Alexander Nevski*, which he has just completed.

SERGEI S. PROKOFIEV

★

B. 1891 in the Ukrainian village of Sontzovka, near Ekaterino-slav (now Dniepropetrovsk), son of an agricultural estate manager; began to compose as a child of five small piano pieces, which were written down by his mother, who also gave him piano lessons; "At six I wrote down myself a valse, a march and a rondo, and I composed a march for four hands when I was seven" he relates in his autobiography; at eight began writing a children's opera *The Giant*, and then the opera *On the Lonely Islands*, which attracted the attention of Sergei Taneev, and caused him to entrust the boy's musical training to his pupil, Reinhold Glier; in 1904 was admitted to the St. Petersburg Conservatoire, where he studied composition under Rimsky-Korsakov, Anatole Liadov and Joseph Vitol, conducting under Nicolai Tcherepine and pianoforte under Anna Esipova; graduated from the Conservatoire in the spring of 1914 in all three subjects, and was awarded the Rubinstein Medal for his own performance of his First Piano Concerto.

At that time he was already the author of numerous works, among them his Second Concerto, which he played for the first time in 1913, the operas *Undina* and *Magdalena*, and other symphonic, piano and vocal compositions. He was already turning his eyes to "the music of to-morrow". "In my opinion", he writes, "it is a mistake for a composer to favour simplification." A warm friendship existed between him and Vladimir Maya-kovsky. In 1918 the poet presented him with a book of his poems, bearing the following ironical inscription: "To the President of the Music Section of the Universe—from the President of the Poetry Section of the Universe." Their contempt for all that was dated for routine, inertness and shallowness in art, brought the two "Presidents" together in their struggle for the art of the new era.

43

Between 1914 and 1918 he composed three Sonatas, several dozens of pieces for piano, the "Classical Symphony" (1917), the opera *The Gambler*, the cantata "Seven of Them", the "Scythian Suite", etc.

His music is impressive in its virility, optimistic joy of living, rhythmic elasticity and dynamism. The well-known Scythian Suite (Alla and Lolly) is written as though in protest against the impressionist over-sensitiveness, against the hothouse atmosphere in music. The archaic intonations of this work seem to herald a new dawn—the revival in our age of man's early joyful approach to nature. The same call to vigour and courage rings in his other compositions; it alternates with lyrical moods and sharp sarcasm, scoffing at the conventions of life and the hypocrisy of society— a derision which is obvious in one of his early operas *The Gambler*, after Dostoyevsky's story.

In 1918 he went abroad. He made many appearances on concert platforms in Europe, Asia, America and Africa, and his operas and ballets were widely produced, among them the *Love of Three Oranges*. After the first night of *Love of Three Oranges*, produced in Chicago, his ballet *Buffoon* was produced in Paris by Sergei Diaguilev; this was followed by the ballets *Le Pas d'Acier* and *The Prodigal Son*. In the ballet *Le Pas d'Acier* he turned, for the first time, to Soviet themes, dealing with the building of a new life in the Russian village. One of his major works during this period was the opera *The Flaming Angel*, after the novel by Valery Biusov, from the music of which was born the Third Symphony. To this period also belongs the Fourth Symphony (based on the music of *The Prodigal Son*), the Fourth Concerto for Piano, the First String Quartet, a cycle of pieces for piano "Things in Themselves", "Reflections", etc.

In 1933 he returned to Russia and began to work on new compositions. He wrote the music to the film "Lieutenant Kije" and to the production of "Egyptian Nights" at the Taivor Chamber Theatre, the music to the film "Alexander Nevsky" by Sergei Eisenstein (and a cantata on the material of this music), the ballet *Romeo and Juliet*, the operas *Semen Kotka* (under the influence of Valentine Kataeev's *Went a Soldier to the Front*) and

44

Betrothal in a Monastry (after the comedy by Sheridan), the ballet *Zolushka*, the Sixth, Seventh and Eight Sonatas for piano, instrumental songs, choruses, ballads, etc.

On 21st December, 1939, on J. Stalin's sixtieth birthday, his new work, the cantata "Zdravitza" for chorus and orchestra, with words in the Russian, Ukrainian, Byelorussian, Kurd, Mari and Mordov languages was performed.

Without taking into account the "Hebrew Overture", his first orientation towards folklore, caused by the stirrings of nostalgia, is seen in two arrangements of Russian songs "White Snow" and "The Guelder Rose", written prior to his return to the fatherland. Back in Russia, he has strengthened his bond with his native people, with its aspirations, feelings and experiences, its vivid and expressive art. He draws from the source of popular music, which permeates the compositions of his later period, and derives inspiration from the heroic life of the people.

In the cantata "Alexander Nevsky", dedicated to the events of past centuries, and in the opera *Semyon Kotka*, dealing with the years of the Civil War in the Ukraine in recent tines, he makes a direct approach to patriotic themes and to the heroism and greatness of the Russian people.

The first symphonic composition which appeared in Soviet music after the outbreak of hostilities was a suite by Prokofiev entitled "The Year 1941". It was followed by the Second Quartet on Kabardinian melodies and the opera *War and Peace*, based on Tolstoi's novel. At the same time, Prokofiev began to work on the music to Eisenstein's new film "Ivan the Terrible".

LEV N. REVUTZIN

*

B. 1889 in the Ukrainian hamlet Yrjovetz, near Poltava; received his initial musical training at home, learning to play the piano; later became a pupil of the Ukrainian composer Nicolai Lissenko and finally studied composition at the Kiev Conservatory under Glier; in 1924 began his educational activity, first at the Kiev Musical and Dramatic Institute named after Lissenko, and later at the Conservatoire.

After working on his First Symphony (which remained in a fragmentary form) and writing a number of piano and vocal compositions, as well as arrangements of Ukrainian folksongs, he completed in 1929 his Second Symphony, which was awarded a prize in the musical contest of the Soviet Republics held in the same year; in a revised form the same symphony won the Stalin Prize in 1941. It was followed by a Concerto for piano and orchestra, several cycles of solo and choral arrangements of Ukrainian folksongs, many of them for mass choirs, including the "Song to Stalin" written to words by the Ukrainian poet Maxime Rilskov.

In 1938 he was awarded the Order of the Red Banner and in 1941 the title of People's Artist of the U.S.S.R. His early compositions, in particular those for piano, are evidently influenced by Tchaikovsky and Rachmaninov. At a later stage, he turned to Ukrainian folksong. One of Revutzin's merits is to have edited and put the final touches to many works of the Ukrainian composers Lissenko (the opera *Taras Bulba*, fragments of Sappho, etc.) and Victor Kossenko (pianoforte concerto and others).

YURI A. SHAPORIN

★

B. 1889, near Chernigov, in the small town of Glukhov, which in the eighteenth century was one of the centres of music of the Ukraine; received his secondary and higher education in St. Petersburg, where he graduated from the Law Faculty of the University; 1913 entered the Conservatoire; graduated in 1918 as composer and conductor, his teachers being Nicolai Sokolov, Maximilian Steinberg and Nicolai Cherepnin; turned, on leaving the Conservatoire to creative and social musical work, concentrating exclusively on theatre music; founded together with Maxime Gorky and Alexander Blok, the Great Dramatic Theatre of Leningrad, and devoted much time to writing music for plays produced on its stage, as well as in other Leningrad theatres; 1926 spent several months in Western Europe acquainting himself with the latest achievements of musical culture, and on his return to the U.S.S.R. continued his work in dramatic theatres; at the same time began to engage in other forms of composition; 1932 completed his First Symphony in Four Parts.

Then followed his cycle of settings or verses by Pushkin and Alexander Blok; 1937 moved to Moscow, and shortly afterwards completed his Symphonic Cantata "On the Fields of Kulikov", written for chorus, solo and orchestra to Alexander Blok's poem; this work was awarded the Stalin Prize in 1941.

At present, he is working on a great historical opera *The Decembrists*, which he began not long before the outbreak of war. Whilst his First Symphony evokes in the listeners' mind the legendary figures of Russian epos, and his Symphonic Cantata resounds with the heroic struggle of the Russian people against the Tartars, routed by Count Dimitri Donsky on the fields of Kulikov, in his new opera he turns to the events of 1825 and to the conflict then raging between the progressive elements in the country and Russian autocracy.

47

VISSARION I. SHEBALIN

★

B. 1902 in the distant Siberian town of Omsk, son of a teacher; musical talent apparent at early age, but received no systematic tuition until ten years old, at first at home and later at the Omsk School of Music, where in addition to piano-playing he studied the theory of music; 1923 came to Moscow and entered the Conservatoire; he graduated in 1928, studying under Nicolai Miaskovsky; immediately on graduation began teaching in the very same institution, and in the Gnessin School of Music. Among his pupils is the composer, Tikhon Khrennikov; 1941, the title of Doctor of Science (research in arts) was added to his professorship. His first works were written in 1921. In the course of the twenty years which followed he produced symphonic, vocal and chamber music, as well as scores for theatre productions, such as his music to the *Dame aux camelias*, and to the films "Torn Boots", "Gobsek", "Front-line Comrades", etc.

His compositions reveal an organic link with Russian classical music, above all with the music of Borodin. These influences come to light already in his first symphony, completed in 1925. On the other hand, in his sonatas for piano, written somewhat later, it is possible to detect features of West-European expressionism. The musical structure of the compositions show points of contact with folksong, and his creative work is enriched by the harmonies and polyphonies of popular music.

His work since the outbreak of war has been intense; in the first months of the war he wrote the Dramatic Overture for Orchestra and subsequently his Fifth Quartet on Slavonic themes. In August, 1942, his comic opera *The Embassy Bride-groom*, on a subject from the period of Catherine II, was produced for the first time in Sverdlovsk. At present he is completing a concerto for violoncello and orchestra and is engaged in the preparatory work for his Fifth Symphony.

48

DIMITRI D. SHOSTAKOVITCH

★

B. 1916 in St. Petersburg; showed talent for music from early childhood; taught by his mother, herself a fine pianist, when nine; 1919 entered the St. Petersburg Conservatoire, studied piano playing under Leonid Nikolaiev until 1923, and theory of composition under Maximilian Steinberg until 1925; his diploma work was his First Symphony, which was publicly performed for the first time on 12th May, 1926, in the Great Hall of the Leningrad Conservatory. It met with an instantaneous success, and laid the foundation for his fame throughout the world.

On leaving the Conservatoire he devoted himself to creative work. Nearly every year brought new compositions, of the most varied types. The First Symphony was followed by a second—"Dedicated to October"—on the occasion of the tenth anniversary of the October Revolution, and a third—"The First of May". Then appeared his compositions for piano—a Sonata, "Three Phantastic Dances"—"Aphorisms"—twenty-four Preludes—songs, octet, etc.

In 1928–9 he wrote his first opera *The Nose*, after the story by Nicolai Gogol, and towards the end of 1930 began working on his second opera *Lady Macbeth of Mtsensk*, after Nikolai Leskov's novel *Katherine Ismailova*, which he completed in December, 1932. This opera was produced on the stage of many theatres in the Soviet Union, as well as in Western Europe and America, and was strongly criticized in the Soviet press for the musical tendency which the composer adopted at the time; he became engrossed in the extreme modernism of West-European music, and his compositions began to show traits such as a freakish distortion and an excessive sharpening of the means of expression. In the beginning of 1936 there appeared in *Pravda* critical articles on *Lady Macbeth* and on the then recently completed ballet *Clear Brooks*. These articles contained a number of interesting state-

49

ments of principle on the subject of the realistic orientation of Soviet art, and a warning against the danger of even the most talented artists succumbing to the temptation of destroying the realities of life in their creative work. Realism in art can have an infinite variety of forms of expression and styles—both "right" and "left"—but will admit of no falsehood. Innovations in art must be warranted by a new intrinsic element in the creative work, and not be a mere predominance of a formal novelty. The foundation of truthfulness in art lies in the close bond between the artist and contemporary life. Such a bond existed in the case of Shostakovitch, as is convincingly shown in his music to the films "Golden Mountains", "Alone", "Comrades", "The New Babylon", "The Encounter" (the theme song of this film became one of the favourites of Soviet youth), "The Youth of Maxime", "The Return of Maxime", "The Chosen Land", "Courtship", "Great Citizens". "Friends", "The Man with the Gun", etc. The enumeration of these films proves that the composer always concerned himself with themes and subjects which were near to his contemporaries, to the whole Soviet people and to its art.

In the compositions which followed ''Katherine Ismailova — Sonata for Violincello, Concerto for Piano, and the Fourth Symphony, he abandoned the expressionist grotesque, the formalistic "aberrations" of youth. In 1937 he composed his Fifth Symphony. "The central figure of my work is Man, with the fullness of his emotional life, and the Finale resolves the tragic and tense strains of the first parts into optimism and joy of living", wrote Shostakovitch about this symphony, which was followed by a String Quartet called "Springtime". Subsequently Shostakovitch produced the Sixth Symphony, in which, in his own words, he "desired to convey the mood of spring, joy, and youth".

1940 brought a new work: his Quintet for Piano and Strings, which was awarded the Stalin Prize in the following year. He had already been previously decorated with the Order of the Red Workers' Banner. Within a short space of time this Quintet has been performed in many towns of the U.S.S.R., with the participation of its composer, who is a fine pianist, having won the Chopin Prize at the All Union Contest of Pianists in 1927.

In the bitter days of the war, he has shown great courage and patriotism; he enrolled in the Home Guard of Leningrad for the defence of his beloved city from the enemy. But he soon passed from defence to attack, and dealt the enemy a severe blow by writing his Seventh Symphony in besieged Leningrad. This Symphony reveals images of two worlds: the world of noble human aspirations, of love, joy and creative labour—and the other world, the world of heartless destruction, mechanized barbarism, and death.

In 1942 he won the Stalin Prize for the second time—for his Seventh Symphony, which was performed throughout the Soviet Union, as well as abroad. At present, he is working on a new composition for the twenty-fifth anniversary of the October Revolution.

VLADIMIR V. SHTCHERBATCHEV

★

B. 1889 in Warsaw, received his musical training at the St. Petersburg Conservatoire, which he entered in 1908 to study piano playing; enrolled a year later in the course for the theory of composition, where for five years he was a pupil of Anatole Liadov and Maximilian Steinberg; graduated from the Conservatoire in 1914.

His early work shows an affinity to the School of Rimsky-Korsakov, to which both his teachers belonged. The two symphonic poems, written in 1913, "A March" and "A Tale", are pervaded with the influence of classical music. Already in the First Symphony, however, composed in the year when he left the Conservatoire, modern tendencies break through.

Musical symbolism was another stage in his evolution. Although the external means of expression of that period contain certain features of French impressionism, in particular in the sphere of vocal music, yet in mood and spirit his music is very akin to the poetry of the Russian poet Alexander Blok. This is shown in the Second Symphony and the suite for piano "From Alexander Blok", as well as in the cycle of songs to the poet's verses.

His Third Symphony, on the other hand, shows distinct traits which are attributable to West-European expressionism, and at the same time constitutes a turning point in the composer's musical development. It plays a role similar to that of the poem "Twelve" in the development of Alexander Blok.

Musical symbolism became a thing of the past. To this new period belong all his latest works, in particular the Fourth Symphony, dedicated to the construction of the Izhorsk foundery, a symphonic oratorio, written for a large orchestra, solo and chorus. His score for films like "Thunderstorm", "The Baltic" and "Peter the Great" emphasizes the new trend. His last composition "Anna Kolossova" is dedicated to the tragic figure of the great Russian actress.

His social and educational activity began when he was still a student; as a young pianist he directed the ballet ensemble of S. Diaguilev. After the October Revolution, he was put in charge of the Musical Section of the Peoples' Commissariat for Education, and carried into effect far-reaching reforms in the field of musical education. He also worked in dramatic theatres, and from 1924 to 1931 held the appointment of Professor of Music at the Leningrad Conservatoire. From 1931 to 1932 he held a chair at the Tiflis Conservatoire, but participated at the same time in the direction of the Leningrad Association of Composers, of which he was elected president in 1937.

G. Popov, V. Tomilin, G. Kiladze, A. Stepanyan, E. Mravinsky are among the many composers who were pupils of Shtcher-batchev.

ARO L. STEPANYAN

★

B. 1897 in Elisabethopol, now renamed Kirovobad; received his initial musical training in his childhood, and when still in his 'teens began to teach music in the Armenian School of Elisabethopol and later at the Armenian School in Alessandropol; acquired his specialized musical education in the Moscow School of Music under Glier and Gnessin, and in the Leningrad Conservatoire from which he graduated in 1930, having completed Professor Shtcherbatchev's course in the theory of composition; returned in the same year to his native land and settled in Everan, the capital of Armenia, where he continues his creative activity to this day.

Intimately acquainted with the folklore and national song of Armenia, he has written a series of compositions which are deeply rooted in the native art of his country. His first opera *Kadz Nazar* (*Nazar the Brave*) is based on the Armenian satirical legend (a variation of story of the brave tailor, and a curious example of the migration of popular tales) and abounds in humorous and grotesque episodes. His second opera *Sasunzi David* is of an entirely different nature. It is an attempt to represent, in terms of music and drama, the heroic and immortal epos of Armenia. Concurrently with his work on both operas, he wrote a large number of symphonic compositions as well as chamber music.

In the spring of 1938 his third opera *Lusabazin* (*The Dawn*) was produced for the first time. It is dedicated to the events of May, 1920—the struggle of the workers and peasants of Armenia against their enemies, the Dashnaks. In 1939, during the celebrations of the first decade of Armenian music in Moscow, this opera was performed with great success in the capital of the Soviet Union. On the same occasion he was awarded the Order of the Red Workers' Banner, having been elected deputy to the Supreme

Soviet of the U.S.S.R. The Armenian Government conferred upon him the title of People's Artist.

Since the outbreak of war, new patriotic songs by him have made their appearance.

MAXIMILIAN O. STEINBERG

★

B. 1893 in Vilno; received secondary education and graduated from the St. Petersburg University; learned to play the violin at home, and continued at the St. Petersburg Conservatoire from 1901–8; was a pupil of Rimsky-Korsakov (whose daughter he subsequently married), Anatole Liadov, and Alexander Glasunov, their influence being predominant in his early works.

During the decade preceding the October Revolution, his music derives inspiration from universal subjects and problems; it also reflects the influence of Skriabin and the French Impressionists. This background is apparent in his Second Symphony, the ballet-triptych "Metamorphoses" on a theme by Ovid (the scenery of which was designed with the collaboration of the well-known painter Bakst) in the dramatic poem "Heaven and Earth" to the words of Byron and in the overture to the production of Maeterlinck's drama *Princess Malen*. It comes to light with particular emphasis in the dramatic phantasy for orchestra, inspired by the first and last scenes of Ibsen's *Brand* with its pathetic finale, depicting the hero's claim to the snow-covered mountain peak and his tragic death under an avalanche of ice.

After the October Revolution he wrote a series of compositions, among them the Third Symphony, a comprehensive arrangement of the national songs of many peoples of the U.S.S.R. for voice and orchestra, the Fourth Symphony—"Turksib"—dedicated to the builders of the famous railway line hundreds of miles across the desert. One of the composer's last works—the ballet *Till Eulenspiegel* on Charles de Coster's subject (the theme for Lev Knipper's sinfonietta and Igor Boelza's opera)—is inspired by the figure of the Flemish national hero, an avenger of his people and the dread of its enemies.

His pupils at the Conservatoire include Shostakovitch, Shtcherbatchev, Shaporin, Popov, and Pastchenko.

56

After the death of Rimsky Korsakov, Steinberg completed and revised his late master's handbooks on orchestration and harmony, and edited them.

In 1938 he was honoured with the Order of Red Workers' Banner.

EUGEN K. TIKOTZY

★

B. 1893 in Petersburg, son of a naval officer; began playing the piano at the age of eight; 1908 entered the School of Music, which he finished in 1912; composed an orera on the subject of Gogol's poetic work "The Eve of St. John"; later, whilst working on pieces for pianoforte and songs, he wrote fragments of symphonies; after completing his secondary education, studied for three years in the St. Petersburg Institute for Psychological and Neurological Research (1911–14) and also in the Arts Faculty of the University, from which however he did not graduate.

During the first World War he served as a company commander on the Russo-German front, and, although wounded by a heavy shell splinter, he remained at his post and took part in General Brussilov's offensive in 1916. Following his demobilisation in 1917, he returned to St. Petersburg for a short while and began studying at the Institute for Geography, but in 1918 he resumed military service and spent six years in the ranks of the Red Army on staff work, which he combined with the study of music and composition. During that period he wrote Red Army songs and choruses as well as variety songs for clubs, etc.

From 1920 onwards his army unit was stationed in Byelorussia, and his first acquaintance with Byelorussian national music dates back to those days. He studied and noted the score of popular songs, of which he wrote arrangements, and when his term of military service expired in 1924, he decided to remain in Byelorussia. His first composition there was the First Symphony in Four Parts, on which he worked for three years, and which is based on themes of popular melodies. In 1927 he founded the School of Music in Bobrusk, which he subsequently directed, without however interrupting his creative work. In 1931, he turned his attention to theatre music and wrote the musical score of over thirty productions in various Byelorussian theatres.

In 1934, he moved to Minsk, the capital of Byelorussia, where he continued his creative and pedagogical work. There he wrote from 1934–9 numerous songs for solo and orchestra, among them "The Storm Petrel" to verses by Maxim Gorki, "Monologue of the Avaricious Knight" to Pushkin's poem "As though it only happened yesterday" to words by Ianka Kupal, etc. In 1938–9, he wrote his opera *Mikhas of the Mountain* (libretto by Piatrus Brovky) and in 1941 his Second Symphony in four parts. In these compositions the national style of Byelorussian music, emerging from the country's folklore, asserts itself fully.

In 1940 the Soviet Government bestowed upon him the Order of the Red Worker's Banner. In the following year, after the outbreak of the war with German fascism, the composer moved to Moscow. In one year of war he has written over twenty patriotic songs and ballads, and commenced working on an opera dedicated to Byelorussian partisans.

S. N. VASSILYENKO

★

B. 1872 in Moscow, where he received secondary and university education; showed interest in music while still in school and took private lessons from Grechaninov and Konius; 1895 entered the Moscow Conservatoire from which he graduated upon completing the course of composition under Taneev and Ippolitov-Ivanov; when still at school wrote music to Euripides' "Alcestis" and during his years of study in the Conservatoire wrote several bigger works—symphonic poem "Three Bloody Battles" (to verses by Alexei Tolstoy), "Epic Poem", string quartet, and others; his diploma work was the cantata "Legend of the great city of Kitezh and the quiet lake Svetoyar"; later, an opera emerged from the musical material of this cantata; 1905 he started teaching in the Moscow Conservatoire, of which he still is a professor; has also acted as conductor and has done extensive work in the field of history of music and ethnography.

His output is rich in variety of theme and genre. For his numerous operas, ballets, symphonic and chamber music, he has made use of the folklore of many peoples. In addition to arrangements of Russian folk songs, used also in some of his bigger works (First Symphony "Legend", opera *Suvorov*, etc.) he has composed series of Marii songs, arrangements of Cingalese, Indian and Japanese melodies for vocal execution accompanied by instrumental ensembles; Chinese and Turkmen suites for orchestra, suite "Soviet East", march-fantasy on themes of Cossack songs, cycles of arrangements of French composers of fourteenth-eighteenth centuries, and many others.

His creative personality is the result of the interweaving of several influences, those of the "mighty handful" (especially Borodin), of Chaikovsky, of French impressionists and, partly, of contemporary West-European music.

The Soviet Government bestowed on him the Order of the Red Banner and awarded him the title of Merited Worker of Arts.

60

ASSAF ZEINALLY

★

B. 1909 in the city of Derbent, Azerbaijan, of peasant origin; was strongly attracted by music while still at school; used to sing and to listen to the Azerbaijan songs, and played the clarinet in the school orchestra; 1923 entered the Baku Musical School; learned to play the trumpet and, later, the piano and 'cello as well, studying at the same time theory of composition under the Azerbaijan composer Uzeir Gadzhibekov; 1926 he entered the Azerbaijan Conservatoire from which he graduated in 1931 upon completing the course of composition under Professor Boris Karagichev.

After a few months in Leningrad, Assaf Zeinally took up teaching in the Azerbaijan Conservatoire. He composed a great deal, but his untimely death interrupted his creative work while he was collecting and studying folklore in Karabakh.

All his works testify to his close relationship with the national songs of Azerbaijan. Although he was unable to complete many of his projects (he left, for instance, drafts of an unfinished symphony), there remain a number of compositions in almost all genres. He did a great deal for the Azerbaijan Dramatic Theatre, whose musical director he was appointed while still a student of the Conservatoire.

BIBLIOGRAPHY

★

A. N. ALEXANDROV

Orchestral Music

Romantic Suite from the music to the play "Ariana and the Blue
  Beard", op 16   (1920, 1928)
Overture on Russian Popular Themes, op 29   (1915, 1930)
Classical Suite from the music to the play "Adrienne Lecouvreur",
  op 32   (1920, 1928)
Ballet Suite, op 37   (1929)
Fragments from an opera, "Forty-first", op 41   (1933–5)
Suite from the music to the play "Don Carlos", op 43   (1933)
Suite from the film "Thirteen", op 47   (1936)
March of the Pioneers   (1933)

Chamber Music

String Quartet, op 7   (1914, 1921)

Pianoforte Music

Sonata, No 1, op 4
Sonata, No 2, op 12
Sonata, No 3, op 18
Sonata, No 4, op 19
Sonata, No 5, op 22
Sonata, No 6, op 26
Sonata, No 7, op 42
Sonata, No 8, op 52
A number of short pieces.

Vocal Music

"Three Goblets", Suite in three parts, for baritone and orchestra
  (or piano), text by N. Tikhonov, op 53   (1942)
Songs to words by Pushkin, Baratinsky, Kuzmin, Fet, Balmont,
  Blok, Yessenin, and others.

Children's Songs, including the cycles "Construction", "Dooda",
  etc.

Theatre Music
Incidental music to the following plays:
"Bacchantes", by Euripides
"Adrienne Lecouvreur", by Scribe
"Ariana and the Blue Beard", by Maeterlinck
"Romeo and Juliet", by Shakespeare
"Nôtre Dame de Paris", by Victor Hugo
"Don Carlos", by Schiller.

A. V. ALEXANDROV

Orchestral Music
Symphony in E flat
Symphonic Poem "Death and Life"

Vocal Music
Cantata "Stalin", text by Enyushkin
Song "Stalin", text by S. Alymov
"Hymn of the Bolshevik Party", text by B. Lebedev-Kumach
Red Army Songs:
"You, planes, strike from heaven"
"Trans-Baikalian Chastushky"
"Song of the Second Amur Division"
"Loss of the Chelyushkin"
"Farewell Song"
"Echelon after Echelon"
"Volga Hauler's Song"
"The Blue Night"
"Life has grown easier"
Red Army Songs, written during the war:
"Patriotic War"
"We Start the Campaign"
"Blow for Blow"
"Again the Storms of War"
"Guardsmen's Song"
Folk-Song Arrangements

Opera
"Water Nymph"

63

B. V. ASSAVIEV

Orchestral Music
Symphony, No 1
Symphony, No 2
Symphony, No 3, "The Fatherland" (written during the war)
Symphony, No 4, "The Seasons of the Year" (written during the
    war)
Sinfonietta, dedicated to the Red Army (written during the war)
"Suvorov Suite" for Wind Orchestra (written during the war)
Concerto for Pianoforte and Orchestra

Chamber Music
String Quartet
Sonata for Viola Solo
Sonata for Trumpet and Pianoforte
Six Arias for Cello and Pianoforte (written during the war)

Piano Music
Four Cycles of Pianoforte Pieces, including "Landscapes" on
    themes of Russian popular songs
Nocturnes "Night Moods" (written during the war)
Variations on the Preobrazhensky March (written during the war)

Vocal Music
Choruses to folk texts, recorded by Pushkin
Cantata—"Song of Stalin"
More than one hundred songs with pianoforte accompaniment

Opera
"Cinderella" (1906)
"The Snow Queen" (1908)
"The Treasurer's Wife". after Lermontov (1935)
"Minin and Pozharsky"
"Altych Chach, the Girl with Golden Curls" (Tartar Opera)
"The Storm", after Ostrovsky
"Feast during the Plague", after Pushkin
"The Brass Horseman", after Pushkin
"Twenty-years later" (in process of composition)

Ballet

"Darfey"	(1909)
"The White Lily"	(1911)
"Pierrot and a Mask"	(1912)
"The Cunning Florenta"	
"Solveig", after Grieg	(1918)
"The Flame of Paris"	(1931)
"The Fountain of Bakhchissarai", after Pushkin	(1933–4)
"Lost Illusions", after Balzac	(1935–6)
"The Partisan Days"	
"Ivan Bolotnikov"	
"The Beauty is Happy", after Gorky's Story "Makar Chudra"	
"Stepan Rasin"	
"The Night before Christmas", after Gogol	
"Ashik-Kerib", after Lermontov	
"Shulamith"	(1940)

Theatre Music
Incidental Music to the following plays:
  "The Seducer of Seville", by Tirso de Molina
  "Oedipus Rex", by Sophocles
  "The Plot of Fiesco", by Schiller
  "Don Carlos", by Schiller
  "The Servant of Two Masters", by Goldony
  "Macbeth"   ⎫
  "The Merchant of Venice"   ⎬   by Shakespeare
  "Othello"   ⎭

Musicological Works

"Tchaikovsky's Instrumental Works	(1921)
"Studies in Symphonic Form"	(1922)
"Stravinsky"	(1929)
"The Musical Form as a Process"	(1930)
"Russian Music from the Beginning of the nineteenth century"	
	(1931)

Monographs on:
Liszt, Chopin, Rubinstein, Tchaikovsky, Rimsky-Korsakov, Taneiev, Borodin, Skriabin, Glazounov

Written During the First Year of War
"Thoughts and Reflections", (Memoires)

Research into Tchaikovsky's "Eugene Onegin"
"Elements of Musical Intonation", the Second Volume of
  "The Musical Form as a Process"
Liszt
Glinka
Czech Music

V. A. BIELY

Orchestral Music
Suito on Chuvash Popular Themes

Chamber Music
"Poem", for viola and pianoforte   (1921)

Pianoforte Music
Four Preludes   (1922)
Sonata, No 1   (1923)
Sonata, No 2   (1926)
Lyric Sonatina   (1928)
Three Miniatures on Bashkirian Themes   (1939)
Sonata, No 3   (1942)

Vocal Music
"The Hunger March", for chorus and orchestra   (1931)
Poem "The Song of Taras", text by Pervomaisky   (1942)
For Solo Voice and Chorus:
"War", a Cycle   (1929)
"26", in memory of the Baku Commissars   (1926)
"Asseyev"
Two Fragments from the poem "V. I. Lenin" by Mayakovsky
                                                                  (1938)
"Three Roads", text by Shevchenko   (1939)
"Song of the Partisan Girl"   (1938)
"Eaglet"   (1936)
"Slav Suite", text by Stiyensky
(Written during the War)
"Ballad of Captain Gastello"
"The Song of the Brave"

66

STEINBERG

SHEBALIN

SHAPORIN

JPPOLITOV-IVANOV

KILADZE

KABALEVSKY

MAKAROVA

KNIPPER

"Bravo, Boys of the Red Navy"
"Red Cavalry Men"
"Partisans in the Woods"
"Song of Five Heroes"

Theatre Music
Incidental music for the plays:
  "Greetings"
  "Spain", etc.

A. V. BOGATYREV

Chamber Music
Trio for violin, cello, and pianoforte   (1935)
String Quartet   (1941)

Pianoforte Music
Variations
Suite "Manfred"

Vocal Music
Poem on "The Tale of a Bear", for soloists, chorus, and orchestra
Choruses, songs, and arrangements of folk-songs

Opera
"Two Foscaris", after Byron
"In the Thick Woods of Polesye"   (1937–9)

I. O. DUNAYEVSKY

Orchestral Music
Ballet Suite
Suite on Chinese Themes
For Jazz Orchestra:
"Rhapsody on Song-Themes of the Peoples of the U.S.S.R."
                                                       (1931)
"The Music Shop"   (1932)

Chamber Music
String Quartet
"Requiem", for reader and quintet
Works for violin, piano, and cello

F   67

Vocal Music
Mass-Songs:
 "Song of Stalin"
 "Soviet Fatherland"
 "Kharkovka"
 "Lyric Song"
 "Komsomol Song"
 "Tractor Song"
 "Song of the Volga"
 "Song of Youth"

Ballet

"Rest of a Faun"	(1924)
"Murzilka", Children's Ballet	(1924)

Operettas

"To Ours and to Yours, or Share and Share Alike"	(1924)
"Bridegrooms"	(1926)
"The Knives"	(1928)
"Polar Passions"	(1928)
"Million Langours"	(1932)
"The Golden Valley"	(1937)
"The Road to Happiness"	(1939)

Film Music

"The First Platoon"	(1932)
"Twice Born"	(1933)
"The Merry Boys"	(1934)
"The Golden Lights"	(1934)
"Three Friends"	(1934)
"The Way of a Ship"	(1935)
"Circus"	(1935)
"The Children of Captain Grant"	(1935)
"Beethoven's Concerto"	(1935)
"Seekers of Happiness"	(1937)
"The Happy Bride"	(1937)
"Volga-Volga"	(1938)

Orchestral Music
Russian Overture
Concerto No 1, for pianoforte and orchestra
Concerto, No 2, for pianoforte and orchestra

Pianoforte Music
A number of short works

Vocal Music
Song Cycles for voice and pianoforte, including "Three Songs",
  text by K. Simonov

Opera
"Quiet flows the Don", after Sholokhov   (1932–4)
"Virgin Soil Upturned",   ,,   ,,   (1936–7)
"In the Days of Volochayev"   (1940)
"Storm", after Ostrovsky   (1941)

Theatre and Film Music
Incidental music to many plays and films

U. GADZHIBEKOV

Vocal Music
Arrangements of Popular Songs

Opera
"Leili and Mejnun"   (1908)
"Sheikh Sanan"
"Sheikh Abas"
"Asli and Kerim"
"Rustam and Zakhrob"
"Arun and Leila"
"Ker-Oglu"

Operetta
"Arshin—Mal—Allan"

Musicological Works
Text books, manuals, and theoretical works

69

R. M. GLIER

Orchestral Music

Symphony, No 1, op 8	(1899–1900)
Symphony, No 2, op 25	(1907)
Symphonic Poem "The Sirens", op 33	(1908
Symphony, No 3, "Ilya Muromets", op 42	(1909–11)
Symphonic Poem "Cossacks of Zaporozh", op 64	(1921)
Symphonic Poem "Trizna", op 66	(1915)
Fantasia for Wind Orchestra, written for the Festival of the Comintern	(1924)
Red Army March, for wind orchestra	(1924)
"Imitation of Ezekiel", for narrator and orchestra	(1919)
"Heroic March of the Buriat-Mongolian ASSR", op 71	(1936)
"Solemn Overture" for the Twentieth Anniversary of the October Revolution, op 72	(1937)
Symphonic Poem "To the memory of a great people's poet" op 73	(1938)
Concerto for harp and orchestra, op 74	(1938)
Overture "Holiday in Ferghana", op 75	(1940)
Overture "The Friendship of the Peoples" written for the 5th Anniversary of the Stalin Constitution, op 79	(1941)
Overture on Slav Themes	(1941)
Overture "For the Happiness of the Fatherland"	(1942)
Concerto for voice and orchestra	(1942)

Chamber Music

String Sextet, op 1	(1900)
String Quartet, op 2	(1900)
Romance for violin and pianoforte, op 3	(1902)
"Ballad" for cello and pianoforte, op 4	(1902)
String Octet, op 5	(1900)
String Sextet, No 2, op 7	(1902)
Two pieces for double-bass and pianoforte, op 9	(1903)
String Sextet, No 3, op 11	(1904)
String Quartet, No 2, op 20	(1905)
Two pieces for double-bass and pianoforte, op 32	(1908)
Miscellaneous pieces for various instruments, op 35	(1908)
Eight pieces for violin and cello, op 39	(1909)
Twelve easy pieces for violin and pianoforte, op 45	(1909)
Twelve pieces for cello and pianoforte, op 51	(1910)

70

Ten Duos for two cellos, op 53 (1911)
Seven instructive pieces for violin and piano, op 54 (1911)
String Quartet, No 3, op 67 (1928)

Pianoforte Music
175 pieces for two or four hands, op 15, 16, 17, 19, 21, 26, 29, 30, 31, 34, 38, 40, 41, 43, 47, 48, 56, 61.

Vocal Music
"Two Poems"for soprano and orchestra, op 60 (1924)
123 Songs with piano accompaniment, op 6, 10, 12, 13, 14, 18, 22, 23, 24, 27, 28, 36, 37, 44, 46, 50, 52, 55, 58, 59, 62, 63.

Opera
"Shakh-Senem", op 69 (1923–34)
"Leili and Mejnun" (1940)

Ballet
"Chrysis", Ballet-Pantomime (1912)
"Cleopatra", Ballet-Mimodrama (1925)
"Comedians", op 68 (1922, 1930)
"Red Poppy", op 70 (1926–7)

Theatre Music
Incidental music to the following plays:
  "Oedipus Rex", by Sophocles (1921)
  "Lysistrata", by Aristophanes (1923)
  "Marriage of Figaro", by Beaumarchais (1927)
  "Hulsara", Uzbek Drama

M. F. GNESSIN

Orchestral Music
"Symphonic Fragments", after Shelley, op 4 (1906–8)
"Songs of Adonis", op 20 (1919)
Symphonic Fantasia in Jewish style, op 30 (1919)
Suite "Jewish Orchestra at the Ball of the Town-Bailiff", from incidental music to the play "Revisor", op 41 (1926)

Chamber Music
"Sonata-Ballade" in C sharp minor, for cello and pianoforte,
    op 7 (1909)
"Requiem" for String Quartet, op 11 (1913–4)
Variations on a Jewish Popular Theme, for String Quartet,
    op 24 (1916)
Sonata in G minor, for violin and pianoforte, op 43 (1928)
Azerbaidjan Folk-Songs, for String Quartet, op 45 (1930)
"Adygeya", Sextet for violin, viola, cello, clarinet, horn, and
    pianoforte, op 48 (1933)

Pianoforte Music
"Songs of Adygeya", for pianoforte duet, op 53

Vocal Music
"Two Songs" with pianoforte, text by Pushkin, op 3
"Ruth", Dramatic Song for voice and orchestra, op 6 (1909)
"Vrubel", Symphonic Dithyramb, text by Bryussov, op 8 (1912)
Song-Cycle, text by Balmont, op 5
"Dedications" to verses by V. Ivanov, Balmont, and Sologub,
    op 10
"The Conqueror Worm", for voice and orchestra, op 12 (1913)
"Rose Garden", text by V. Ivanov for voice and piano, op 15
Song-Cycle, text by Alexander Blok, op 16
Song-Cycle, text by Sologub, op 22
Song-Cycle, text by Contemporary Poets, op 26
"1905–1917", Symphonic Monument, for soloists, chorus and
    orchestra, text by Yessenin, op 40 (1925)
"Two Songs of Laura", text by Pushkin, op 51
"Amangeldy", heroic song to text by Djambul, op 55 (1940)
Arrangements of Jewish Folk-songs for voice and pianoforte,
    op 32, 33, 34, 42.

Opera
Opera-Poem "Youth of Abraham", op 36 (1921–3)

Theatre Music
Incidental music to the plays
    "Antigone", by Sophocles, op 13 (1909–15)
    "The Rose and the Cross", by Blok, op 14 (1914)

"Phoenician Women", op 17	(1912–6)
"Oedipus Rex", by Sophocles, op 19	(1914–5)
"The Controller", by Gogol, op 41	(1926)
"Red-haired Motele", by Utkin, op 44	(1926–9)

M. M. IPPOLITOV-IVANOV

Orchestral Works

Symphonic Poem "Yar-Khmel", op 1	(1882)
"Caucasian Sketches", op 10	(1894)
Symphonic Poem "Iberia", op 42	(1894–5)
Symphony, No 1, op 46	(1907)
"Armenian Rhapsody", op 48	(1894–5)
"On the Volga", for small orchestra, op 50	
Symphonic Poem "Mtsyry", after Lermontov, op 54	(1923–4)
"Turkish March", op 55	
"From Ossian", Three Musical Tableaux, op 56	
"Episode from Schubert's Life", op 61	(1928)
"Turkish Fragments", op 62	
Suite "In the Steppes of Turkmenia", op 65	
"Voroshilov March", op 67	
"Musical Scenes of Uzbekistan", op 69	
Symphonic Poem "The Year 1917", op 71	
"Catalonian Suite", op 79	(1934)
Symphony "Kardis" (his last work)	(1935)

Chamber Music

Sonata for violin and pianoforte, op 8
String Quartet, No 1, op 9
String Quartet, No 2, op 13
"Confession" for cello and pianoforte, op 19
"Romantic Ballade" for violin and pianoforte, op 20
"An Evening in Georgia", for harp, flute, oboe, clarinet, and
    bassoon, op 69a

Pianoforte Music

Five short pieces for pianoforte, op 7

Vocal Music

Songs with pianoforte, op 3, 4, 5, 11, 14, 15

"Alsatian Ballad" for mixed chorus unaccompanied, op 15a
Ten choruses for female voices with pianoforte, op 16
Five choruses for mixed voices, op 17
Five characteristic pieces for chorus and orchestra or pianoforte, op 18
Songs with pianoforte, op 21, 22, 23
"The Legend of the White Swan", for mixed chorus unaccompanied, op 24
Cantata "In Memory of Pushkin", for children's voices and pianoforte, op 26
Songs with pianoforte, op 27, 28, 31, 33
Five Poems for Children's Choir, op 32
Cantata "In Memory of Zhukovsky", for mixed chorus and pianoforte, op 35
"Pythagorean Hymn to the Rising Sun", mixed chorus, 10 flutes, 2 harps and clarinet, op 39
Cantata "In Memory of Gogol", for children's chorus and pianoforte, op 47
Fifteen Children's Choruses, op 51
"Hymn to Labour", for mixed chorus and orchestra, op 59 (1927)

Opera
"Ruth"   (1887)
"Azra", Biblical Scenes, op 6   (1888)
"Assya", Lyrical Scenes, op 30   (1899)
"Treachery", op 43   (1908–9)
"Ole from Norland", op 53   (1916)
"Marriage, 2nd, 3rd, and 4th Acts to Moussorgsky's unfinished opera, op 70   (1931)
"The Last Barricade", op 74   (1933–4)

D. B. KABALEVSKY

Orchestral Music
Pianoforte Concerto, No 1, in A minor   (1929)
Symphony, No 1 in C sharp minor   (1932)
Symphony, No 2 in E minor   (1934)
Symphony, No 3, "Requiem", in B flat mnor   (1933)
Pianoforte Concerto, No 2 in G minor   (1936)
"The Comedians", Suite for small orchestra   (1940)

Chamber Music
String Quartet in A minor   (1929)

Pianoforte Music
Sonata
Two Sonatinas
Short easy pieces

Vocal Music
"Poem of Struggle", for mixed choir and orchestra   (1930)
"Our Great Fatherland", Cantata for mixed chorus and orchestra
(1942)
"People's Avengers", Suite for mixed chorus and orchestra (1942)
Songs with pianoforte accompaniment
Children's Songs
Battle Songs

Opera
"The Golden Spikes"   (1940)
"The Craftsman from Clancy", after Romain Rolland's novel
  Colas Brugnon   (1937)
"Before Moscow"   (1942)

Theatre Music
Incidental music to the following plays:
"Measure for Measure", by Shakespeare
"The School for Scandal", by Sheridan
"Madame Bovary", by Flaubert

Film Music
"Aero-city"
"Shtchors"

A. KHACHATURIAN

Orchestral Music
Dance Suite   (1933)
Symphony   (1933–4)
Concerto for pianoforte and orchestra   (1936)
Two Suites from the ballet "Happiness"   (1939)
Concerto for violin and orchestra   (1940)

Three marches for wind orchestra
Two pieces on Uzbek Themes, for wind orchestra
Two pieces on Armenian Themes, for wind orchestra

Chamber Music
String Quartet in C major   (1932)
Trio in G minor for clarinet, violin, and pianoforte   (1932)
Sonata in D minor for violin and piano
"Dance" in B flat major for violin and piano
"Song-Poem" for violin and pianoforte

Pianoforte Music
"Toccata"
"Scherzo"
"Poem"
"Dance"

Vocal Music
"Song of Stalin", Symphonic Poem for mixed chorus and
     orchestra, text by Ashug Mirza from Tausa, Azerbaijan
30 miscellaneous vocal works
War Songs, including:
     "Captain Gastello"
     "March of the Guardsmen"
     "Men from the Urals"

Ballet
"Happiness"   (1939)
"Gayane"   (1942)

Theatre Music
Incidental music to the following plays:
     "Macbeth", by Shakespeare
     "Widow of Valencia", by Lopez-de-Vega
     "The Ruined Home", by Sandunyan

Film Music
"Pepo"
"The Garden"
"Salavat Yulayev"

Orchestral Music

Concerto for pianoforte and orchestra, op 1 (1932–3)
Suite from the incidental music to the play "Mik", by Shestakov,
op 3 (1934)
Symphony in B flat minor, op 4 (1934–5)
Suite from the incidental music to "Much ado about Nothing",
by Shakespeare, op 7 (1935–6)
Symphony, No 2 in C minor, op 9 (1941–2)
Suite from the incidental music to the play "Don Quixote", by
Cervantes, op 10 (1940–42)

Pianoforte Music

Five pieces, op 2
Three pieces, op 5 (1934–5)

Vocal Music

"The Day is near", anti-fascist song (1934)
Three Songs to text by Pushkin, op 6 (1935)
Songs from "Much ado about Nothing", op 7 (1935–6)
Five songs to text by Robert Burns, translated by S. Marshak,
op. 11 (1942)
War Songs:
"We know how to fight", text by Lebedev-Kumach
"Friendship", text by A. Barto
"Song of Moscow", text by V. Gussey
"Song of the Moscow Girl", text by A. Barto
"Farewell", text by Vinnikov
"All for the Fatherland", text by Gussev
"The Town in the North", text by Gussev
"The men from the Urals", text by A. Barto

Opera

"In the Storm", after Wirt's novel *Loneliness*

Theatre Music

Incidental music to the following plays:
"Mik", by Shestakov (1934)
"Much Ado about Nothing", by Shakespeare (1935)
"Don Quixote", by Cervantes (1940)

77

Film Music
"The Swineherdess and the Shepherd"   (1941)

G. V. KILADZE

Orchestral Music
Symphonic Poem "The Hermit"
Suites

Vocal Music
Mass-Choruses, including "Song of Stalin"

Opera
"Lado Ketkhovelli"

Theatre and Film Music
"The Last Masquerade"
"Arsen"

L. KNIPPER

Orchestral Music
Symphony No 1, op 13   (1927)
"Candide", Suite, op 15
Lyric Suite, op 18   (1928)
Suite in Four Movements, op 19   (1928)
Four Children's Miniatures, op 24
Tadjik Suite, op 28   (1931)
"Vanch", Tadjik Suite, op 29
Symphony, No 2, "The Lyrical", op 30   (1932)
Sinfonietta, op 33   (1932)
Suite "Memories", op 31   (1932)
Symphony, No 3, op 32   (1932–3)
Four Études for large orchestra, op 34   (1933)
Symphony, No 4, "Komsomol Fighters", op 41   (1933–4)
Symphony, No 5, op 42   (1933–4)
"Till Eulenspiegel", four Ballet Études, op 43   (1934)
Symphony, No 6 in E   (1938)
Symphonic Poem   (1940)
Turkmenian Sketches   (1940)
Suite "The Ways of Turkmenia"   (1940)

78

Symphonic Suite	(1940)
Fantasies on two Balkar Themes	
Two Preludes on Iranian Themes for small orchestra	(1942)
"Maku", 3 Songs on Kurd Themes, for small orchestra	(1942)
"Sia", Azerbaidjan Dance, ,, ,, ,,	(1942)
Symphony, No 7 in D	(1942)
Concerto for violin and orchestra	(1942)

Vocal Music

Three Russian Folk-Songs for voice and small orchestra, op 35
(1933)
Eight Love Songs, op 45 (1935)
"A Poem to Horses" in memory of Dovator, for mixed chorus
and orchestra (1942)
Mass and battle songs, including "Steppe Cavalry"

Opera

"Candide", op 15	(1926–7)
"North Wind", op 25	(1929–30)
"Maria"	

Ballet

| "Satanella", op 4 | (1924) |
| "The Little Negro Sebi", op 24 | (1931) |

Music to Plays and Films

V. S. KOSSENKO

Orchestral Music
"Heroic Overture"
"Moldavian Poem"
Concerto for pianoforte and orchestra
Concerto for violin and orchestra

Chamber Music
String Quartet
Classical Trio, for pianoforte, violin, and cello
Sonata for violin and pianoforte
Sonata for viola and pianoforte
Sonata for cello and pianoforte

79

Pianoforte Music
Three Sonatas
Eleven Études, in the form of Ancient Dances
"Poetical Legend'"
Two Nocturnes
Two Concert-Waltzes

Vocal Music
Five Ukrainian Folk-Songs, arranged for voice and pianoforte
Four Songs, text by P. Titchin
Battle Songs

M. KOVAL

Orchestral Music
Suite "The Family of Nations"
Suite "From the Life of a Red Army Man"
Poem "Tale of a Partisan"

Vocal Music
"Emilian Pugatchev", Oratorio for soloists, chorus, and or-
    chestra   (1939)
"The People's Sacred War", oratorio for soloists, chorus and
    orchestra
"Chkalov", oratorio for soloists, chorus and orchestra
"Fighting in Moscow", Cantata for chorus and orchestra
Mass-songs and war-songs, including
    Song-Cycle on Lenin and Stalin
    Song-Cycle "Fighters of 1905"
    Song-Cycle "Cursed Past", text by Nekrassov
    Song-Cycle, text by Pushkin
    Song-Cycle "A Front Line Note-book", after Shtchepachev
                                                           (1942)

Opera
"The Manor House", after Pushkin   (1930)
"Emilian Pugachev"   (1939)
"The Wolf and the Seven Goats"   (1939)

Theatre Music
"The Earth is Rising"   (1930)

80

Orchestral Music

Symphonic Poem "Salome", after Oscar Wilde, op 19

Symphonic Fragments "The Rose and the Cross", after Alexander Blok, op 26

Symphony in F sharp minor, op 35   (1925)

Suite "Night on the Old Market Place", from the incidental music to the play by L. Perez, op 38   (1924)

"Mourning Ode", op 40   (1925–6)

"USSR, the Shock Brigade of the World Proletariat", op 40
(1931–2)

Suite on Kabardino-Balkar Themes   (1941)

Chamber Music

"Poem-Quartet", for String Quartet, op 9

"Jewish Sketches", two suites for String Quartet and clarinet in B flat, op 12 and 13   (1909–10)

"Elegy" for violin, cello, and pianoforte, op 16

Minor works for various instruments: op 1, 1a, 2a, 4, 10, 15, 21, 24, 41, 43, 45, 46, 47

Pianoforte Music

Sonata, op 34   (1922)

Dance Suite in Six Movements, op 44   (1934)

Short pieces, op 2, 3, 7, 11, 18, 30, 46, 50

Vocal Music

Songs and ballads for voice and pianoforte, op 5, 5a, 6, 8, 17, 20, 22, 23, 25, 27, 28, 29, 31, 32, 39, 42

"Kaddish", Symphonic Cantata, for solo voice, chorus, and orchestra, op 33   (1921–2)

Ten Jewish Folk-songs, arranged for voice and pianoforte, op 49   (1937–8)

Song-Cycle "From Balkaria's Mountains", text by Tchikovan

"Curse on the enemy"

Opera

"Zagmuk"   (1929–30)

Ballet

"Laurencia"   (1939)

"Tatiana"   (1940–2)
Choral Ballet "Othello and Desdemona"

Music to Numerous Plays and Films

B. V. LIATOSHINSKY

Orchestral Music
Symphony, No 1
Symphony, No 2
"Fantastic March"
Overture on Four Ukrainian Themes
Symphony, No 3 (in process of composition)
Marches for brass orchestra

Chamber Music
Three string quartets
Trio for violin, viola, and pianoforte
Sonata for violin and pianoforte

Pianoforte Music
Two Sonatas, based on Ukrainian Themes
Minor pieces

Vocal Music
"Solemn Cantata" for mixed chorus and orchestra, written for
the Sixtieth Birthday of Comrade Stalin, text by Rilskov   (1938)
Arrangements of Ukrainian Folk-Songs

Operas
"The Golden Hoop"   (1924–36)
"Shtchors"
Together with L. N. Revutsky he has orchestrated Lissenko's
  opera "Taras Bulba".

K. I. LISTOV

Vocal Music
Mass and battle-songs, including:
  "Tachanka", text by Rudermann
  "Baccy",   ,,   ,,   ,,
  "Tidings",   ,,   ,,   ,,

82

ASSAFIEV

BELY

TIKOTZY

REVUTZIN

LIATOSHINSKY   POKRASS

          MURADELI   PASHTCHENKO

"In a Dug-Out", text by Surkov
"Salute to the Men of the Black-Sea Fleet," text by Kracht
   and Stovratzcy
"The Mother's Order", text by Alimov
"Let the Fascists Try", text by Zamiatin
"Reconnaissance", text by Oshania
"Whisper, Oh Willows", text by Shubin

N. V. MAKAROVA

Orchestral Music
Symphony in D minor   (1936)

Chamber Music
Two Melodies for oboe and pianoforte
Sonata for violin and pianoforte
Two Melodies for violin and pianoforte

Pianoforte Music
Sonatina
Six Preludes

Vocal Music
"Cantata to Molotov", for soloists, chorus and orchestra   (1940)
Song-cycle, text by Pushkin
Song-cycle, text by Rustaveli
"Children's Song to Stalin"
Mass-Songs:
   "Falcons"
   "Polar Song "
   "Front-line Comrade"
   "Sailors"
   "Ural Song"
   "You will return to me victorious"

Opera
"Courage"   (1940–2)

Film Music
"The Happy Exchange"
"In the Land of the Dolls"

Orchestral Music

Symphony, No 1 in C minor, op 3	(1908)
Symphonic Poem "Silence", after Edgar Allan Poe, op 9	(1910)
Sinfonietta in A major, op 10	(1911)
Symphony, No 2 in C sharp, op 11	(1912)
Symphonic Poem "Alastor", after Shelley, op 14	(1914)
Symphony, No 3 in A minor, op 15	(1914)
Symphony, No 4 in E minor, op 17	(1918)
Symphony, No 5 in D major, op 18	(1918)
Symphony, No 6 in E flat minor, op 23	(1923)
Symphony, No 7 in B minor, op 27	(1922)
Symphony, No 8 in A major, op 26	(1925)
Symphony, No 9 in E minor, op 27	(1927)
Symphony, No. 10, op 30	(1927)
Serenade for small orchestra in E flat major, op 32, No 1	(1929)
Sinfonietta, No 2 for string orchestra in B minor, op 32, No 2	(1929)
Lyric Concertino for small orchestra in G major, op 32, No 3	(1929)
Symphony, No 11 in B flat minor, op 34	(1932)
Symphony, No 12 in G minor, op 35	(1932)
Symphony, No 13 in B flat minor, op 36	(1933)
Symphony, No 14 in C major, op 37	(1933)
Symphony, No 15, in D minor, op 38	(1934)
Symphony, No 16 in F major, op 39	(1936)
Symphony, No 17 in G sharp minor, op 41	(1937)
Symphony, No 18 in C major, op 42	(1937)
Concerto for Violin and orchestra, op 44	(1938)
Symphony, No 19 for wind orchestra, op 46	(1939)
"Greetings Overture" on the Sixtieth Anniversary of Joseph Stalin, op 48	(1939)
Symphony, No 20 in E major, op 50	(1940)
Symphony, No 21 in F sharp minor, op 51	(1940)
"Symphony-Ballade", No 22 on the Great War of Liberation op 54	(1941)
Symphony, No 23, op 56	(1941)
Symphony, No 24, op 57	(1941)
March for wind orchestra, op 58	(1941)
Overture in G minor for wind orchestra, op 60	(1942)

Chamber Music
Sonata for cello and pianoforte in D major, op 12   (1911)
String Quartet, No 1 in A minor, op 33   (1930)
String Quartet, No 2 in C minor, op 33   (1930)
String Quartet, No 3 in D minor, op 33   (1910)
String Quartet, No 4 in F minor, op 33   (1909–10)
String Quartet, No 5 in E minor, op 47   (1939)
String Quartet, No 6 in G minor, op 49   (1940)
String Quartet, No 7 in F major, op 55   (1941)
String Quartet, No 8 in F sharp major, op 59   (1942)

Pianoforte Music
Sonata, No 1 in D minor, op 6   (1907–9)
Sonata, No 2 in F sharp minor, op 13   (1912)
Sonata, No 3 in C minor, op 19   (1920)
Fancies, op 25   (1917–22)
Sonata, No 4 in C minor   (1925)
"Souvenirs", op 29   (1907–27)
"Yellowed Pages", op 31   (1906–28)
Children's Pieces in Three Books, op 43   (1938)

Vocal Music
Six Songs, text by Baratinsky, op 1   (1907)
Nine Songs, text by Hippius, op 2   (1904–6)
Three Songs,   ,,   ,,   op 4   (1905–8)
Four Songs,   ,,   ,,   op 5   (1904–8)
Five Songs, text by Balmont, op 7   (1908–9)
Four Songs, text by Tiutcheff and V. Ivanoff, op 8   (1908–9)
Six Songs, text by Hippius, op 16   (1913–4)
Five Songs, text by Alexander Blok, op 20   (1921)
Two Songs, text by Tiutcheff, op 21   (1922)
Eight Songs, text by Delvig, op 22   (1925)
Twelve Songs, text by Lermontov, op 40   (1935–6)
Three Sketches for voice and pianoforte, text by Shtchepatchev
    and Kvitky, op 45
Ten Songs, text by Shtchepatchev, op 52
Oratorio "Kirov is with us" (in process of composition)

A. V. MOSSOLOV

Orchestral Music
Concerto for pianoforte and orchestra, No 1 in A minor   (1927)

Symphonic Poem "The Iron Foundry"	(1928)
Symphony, No 1 in C major	(1928)
Concerto for pianoforte and orchestra, No 2 in C major	(1932)
Turkmenian Suite in Three Movements	(1933)
Symphony, No 2 in B minor	(1934)
Uzbek Dance	(1935)
Concerto for cello and orchestra	(1935)
Concerto for harp and orchestra	(1936)
Symphony, No 3 in C minor	(1937)
Symphony, No 4 "To Lermontov"	(1940)

Chamber Music

String Quartet in A minor	(1926)
Sonata for viola and pianoforte	(1928)
Dance Suite for violin, cello, and pianoforte	(1928)

Pianoforte Music
Five Sonatas

Vocal Music
"Kirghiz Rhapsody", for mixed chorus, soloists, and orchestra
(1933)

Songs to texts by Pushkin, Lermontov, and Blok
Mass-songs and battle-songs

Opera

"The Dam"	(1930)
"The Hero"	(1938)
"The Signal"	(1941–2)

V. I. MURADELI

Orchestral Music

Georgian Symphonic Dance	(1936)
Symphony "In Memory of Kirov"	(1938)
"Solemn Overture", dedicated to Molotov	(1940)

Vocal Music

"Our Leader", Cantata for soloists, mixed chorus, and orchestra,	
written for the Sixtieth Anniversary of Joseph Stalin	(1939)
"Song of Stalin's Youth" for voice and orchestra	(1940)

"Zdravitza" for mixed chorus and orchestra (1941)
March for mixed chorus and wind orchestra (1941)
Arrangements for solo voice or chorus of Georgian folk-songs
Battle-songs written during the war:
    "Father and Son"
    "Dovator's Cossacks"
    "Wait for me"

Theatre Music
Incidental music to the following plays: —
    "Honour", by Mdivan
    "The Mountains of Fatusiva"

Film Music
"The Ferghana Canal"

A. F. PASHTCHENKO

Orchestral Music
Symphony, No 1
Symphony, No 2
Symphony, No 3
Symphony, No 4
Symphony, No 5
Symphony, No 6
Symphony, No 7
"Solemn Polonaise"
"Festive Overture"
"The Street is gay" for orchestra of Folk-instruments
"Ukrainian Rhapsody"   ,,   ,,   ,,   ,,
"Oriental Rhapsody"   ,,   ,,   ,,   ,,

Vocal Music
Oratorio "The Liberation of Prometheus"
"Requiem" for chorus and orchestra, to the memory of the heroes
    who have laid down their lives in the Great War of Liberation
                                            (1941–42)

Opera
"The Revolt of the Eagle" (1925)
"Tsar Maximilian" (1927)

87

"The Black Cliff"   (1930)
"Pompadour"   (1936)

Film Music
"Dubrovsky"

Vocal Music
Mass and battle-songs, including
    "Song to Stalin"
    "Moscow"
    "Red Cavalry"
    "If War breaks out to-morrow"
    "The sword will not touch us"
    "The Stormy Clouds"
    "Song of the Oath"

Film Music
"Front-line Comrades"
"A Young Lady with Character"
"If War breaks out to-morrow"
"Worker and Peasant"
"The 20th May"
"A Thought about Cossack Golot"
"The First of May"
"Sons of the Working People"
"Tractor Drivers"

Orchestral Music
"Telescope", Part 1   (1926)
"Telescope", Parts 2 and 3   (1928)
Symphony, No 1 in A major   (1929)
Overture "May 1st"   (1930)
Symphony, No 2 "Moscow"   (1931)
Symphony, No. 3, "The Romantic"   (1932)
Concerto for pianoforte and orchestra in D minor   (1933)
Symphony, No 4 in A major, "The Red Army"   (1933)
"Telescope", Part 4   (1933–5)
Symphony, No 5 in D major   (1940)

| Symphony, No 6 in F major | (1942) |
| "Dance-Riddle" for small orchestra | |

Chamber Music
Trio for violin, cello, and pianoforte	(1936)
"Ila", Suite for wood-wind Quartet	(1931)
Various other instrumental works	

Pianoforte Music
Five Sonatas
Five Suites
"Events", ten pieces	(1931)
"Toccata"	(1939)
Twenty-four Postludes	(1941)
Three Mazurkas	

Opera
"The Irish Hero", after Singer

Music to Children's Plays
"The Negro and the Monkey"	(1927)
"Tale of the Fisherman and the Fish", after Pushkin	(1934–8)
"The Golden Key", after A. Tolstoi	(1936)

G. N. POPOV

Orchestral Music
Symphony	(1928–34)
Two Suites	
Concerto for violin and orchestra	

Chamber Music
Quintet for flute, clarinet, trumpet, cello, and double-bass

Pianoforte Music
Grand Suite
"Expression" and "Melody"

Vocal Music
"Heroic Intermezzo" for solo voice, chorus, and orchestra, on
the symphonic material of the opera "Alexander Nevsky"

89

Opera
"Alexander Nevski"

Film Music
"The New Fatherland"   (1932)
"Chapayev"   (1933–4)

Orchestral Music
Sinfonietta, op 5/48   (1909, 1929)
"Rêves", op 6   (1910)
"Esquisses Automnales", op 8   (1910, 1934)
Piano Concerto, No 1 in D flat, op 10   (1911)
Piano Concerto, No 2 in G minor, op 16   (1913)
Violin Concerto, No 1 in D major, op 19   (1913)
"Scythian Suite", op 20   (1914)
Classical Symphony, op 25
Piano Concerto, No 3 in C major   (1917)
Symphony, No 2, op 40   (1924)
Overture, op 42   (1926)
"Divertissement", op 43   (1925–9)
Symphony, No 3, op 44   (1928)
Symphony, No 4, op 47   (1929–30)
Four Portraits from the opera "The Gambler", op 49   (1931)
Piano Concerto, No 4, for the left hand, op 53   (1931)
Piano Concerto, No 5 in G major, op 55   (1932)
Symphonic Song, op 57   (1933)
Concerto for cello and orchestra, op 58   (1935–8)
Symphonic Suite "Lieutenant Kije", op 60   (1934)
Symphonic Suite "Egyptian Nights", op 61   (1934)
Violin Concerto, No 2 in G minor, op 63   (1935)
"Peter and the Wolf", op 67   (1936)
Marches for Military Band, op 69   (1935)
Russian Overture, op 72   (1936)
Symphonic March, op 88
Symphonic Suite "1941", op 90   (1941)

Chamber Music
"Ballade" for cello and pianoforte, p 15   (1912)

"Overture on Hebrew Themes", for clarinet, string quartet, and
  pianoforte, op 34   (1919)
Quintet for wind and strings, op 39   (1924)
String Quartet, No 1, op 50   (1930)
Sonata for two violins, op 56   (1932)
String Quartet, No 2 on Kabardino-Balkar Themes, op 92

Pianoforte Music
Sonata, No 1 in F minor, op 1   (1909)
Four Études, op 2   (1909)
"Conte, Badinage, Marche Fantome", op 3   (1907–11)
"Reminsicences", op 4   (1908–12)
"Toccata", op 11
Nine pieces, op 12   (1908–13)
Sonata, No 2 in D minor, op 14   (1912)
Cycle "Sarcasms", op 17   (1912–4)
"Visions fugitives", op 22   (1915–7)
Sonata, No 3 in A minor, op 28   (1907–17)
Sonata, No 4 in C minor, op 29   (1908–17)
"Contes de la vielle Grand 'mère", op 31   (1918)
Four pieces, op 32   (1918)
Sonata, No 5, op 38   (1923)
"Choses en soi", op 45   (1928)
Six Pieces, op 52   (1931)
Two Sonatinas, op 54   (1931)
"Promenade, Paysage, Sonatine Pastorale", op 59   (1934)
"Penseés", op 62   (1933–4)
"Musique d'Enfants", op 65   (1935)
Ten pieces from "Romeo and Juliet" op 75   (1937)
Sonata, No. 6, in A flat major, op 82   (1939)

Vocal Music
"Ivan and the Wave", text by Balmont, for double female
  chorus with orchestra, op 7   (1910)
Two Songs, op 9   (1910–1)
"The Ugly Duckling", op 18   (1914)
Five Poems, op 23   (1915)
Five Songs, text by Anna Akhmatove, op 27   (1916)
Five Melodies without words for voice and pianoforte, op 35
                                                           (1920–5)

91

Five Songs, text by Balmont, op 36 (1921)
"Seven, they are Seven", for tenor solo, chorus and orchestra,
    op 30 (1917)
Mais Songs, for chorus, op 66 (1936)
Song "Chatterbox", op 68 (1936)
Songs, text by Pushkin, op 73 (1936)
"Cantata for the twentieth anniversary of the October Revolu-
    tion", to the words of Lenin, Stalin and Marx, for double
    chorus, symphony orchestra, military band and accordion
    band op 75 (1937)
Cantata "Alexander Nevsky", for mezzo-soprano, chorus and
    orchestra, op 70, 1938 (1938)
"Songs of our Days", for chorus and orchestra, op 76 (1937)
Seven Mass Songs, for voice and piano, op 79
"Zdravitza" for mixed chorus and orchestra, text in five
    languages, op 85 (1939)
Ballad "Zolushka" op 87 (1941)

Opera
"Magdalene", op 13 (1911–3)
"The Gambler", op 24 (1916–27)
"The Love of Three Oranges", op 33 (1919)
"The Flaming Angel", op 37 (1922–5)
"Semen Kotko", op 81
"War and Peace", after Tolstoi, op 91 (1941)
"Betrothal in a Monastry", op 86 (1940–1)

Ballet
"Buffoon", op 21 (1915–20)
"Le Pas d'Acier", op 41 (1925)
"L'Enfant Prodigue", op 46 (1928–9)
"Sur le Borysthène", op 51 (1930)
"Romeo and Juliet", op 64 (1935)

Theatre Music
Incidental music to Pushkin's "Eugene Onegin", op 71 (1936)
Incidental music to Pushkin's "Boris Godounov", op 74 (1936)

Film Music
"Alexander Nevsky" (1938)

Orchestral Music
Symphony, No 1
Symphony, No 2
Piano Concerto, No 1
Piano Concerto, No 2

Vocal Music
"Song to Stalin", Cantata for chorus and orchestra, text by
    Rilskov
Arrangements of Ukrainian folk-songs
Battle songs

Music to Plays and Films
Together with B. V. Liatoshinsky he has orchestrated Lissenko's
    opera "Taras Bulba"

Y. A. SHAPORIN

Orchestral Music
Symphony in E minor   (1932–3)
Humorous Suite "The Flea", after Leskov, op 8

Piano Music
Suite, op 5   (1924)
Suite, op 7   (1927)

Vocal Music
Song Cycle, text by Tiutieff, op 6   (1921)
Song Cycle, text by Pushkin, op 10
"Elegies", five songs, text by Russian poets   (1940)
Song Cycle, "Distant Youth", text by Blok, op 12   (1939)
"On the Kulikov Field", Symphonic Cantata for soloists, chorus
    and orchestra, op 14

Opera
"The Decembrists", libretto by A. Tolstoi

Theatre Music
Incidental music to the following plays:
    "The Robbers", by Schiller   (1919)
    "King Lear", by Shakespeare   (1920)
    "The Assault of Perekop",   (1927)

"The Straw Hat", by Labiche   (1920)
"Tartuffe", by Molière   (1929)
"Boris Godounov", by Pushkin   (1934)
"The Marriage of Figaro", by Beaumarchais   (1935)
"A Comedy of Errors", by Shakespeare   (1940)
"The Nobles' Nest", by Turgenev   (1940)

Film Music
"Minin and Pozharsky"   (1939)
"General Suvorov"   (1940)

V. I. SHEBALIN

Orchestral Music
Symphony, No 1 in F minor   (1925)
Symphony, No 2 in C sharp minor   (1929)
Concertino in C major, for horn and small orchestra   (1930)
Symphony, No 3 in C major   (1934–5)
Symphony, No 4 in B flat major   (1935)
Overture on Mari themes   (1936)
Concertino in G major for violin and string orchestra   (1932)
Concerto for violin and orchestra   (1936–40)
Two Suites

Chamber Music
Trio in G minor for violin, viola and cello
String Quartet, No 1 in A minor   (1923)
Suite for violin solo   (1933)
String Quartet, No 2 in B flat major   (1934)
String Quartet, No 3 in E minor   (1939)
String Quartet, No 4   (1940)
Sonatina for violin and viola   (1942)
String Quartet, No 5 on Slav Themes   (1942)

Pianoforte Music
Two Sonatas
Three Sonatinas

Vocal Music
"Lenin", Symphonic Poem to text by Mayakovsky for soloists,
    mixed choir and orchestra   (1931)

94

Cantata "Blue May", text by Asseyev, for mixed chorus and
orchestra
Songs, text by Pushkin, Heine and others
Mass and Battle songs

Theatre Music
Incidental music to the following plays:
"Mary Stuart" and "The Robbers", by Schiller
"A Glass of Water", by Scribe
"Mozart and Salieri", "Dormant Knight", "The Stone
Guest", by Pushkin
"Masquerade", by Lermontov
"On the Banks of the Neva", "Lyubov Yarovaya", by Trenev

Film Music

D. SHOSTAKOVICH
Orchestral Music

Scherzo in F sharp minor, op 1	(1919)
Theme and Variations, op 3	(1921–2)
Scherzo in E flat major, op 7	(1923)
Symphony, No 1, in F minor, op 10	(1925)
Symphony, No 2, "The October", op 14	
"Tahiti Trot", op 16	
Symphony No 3, "The First of May", op 20	
Suite from the Ballet "The Golden Age", op 22	(1930)
Interlude and Finale, op 23	
Suite for Jazz orchestra, op 38	
Suite from the film "The Golden Mountains", op 30	(1931)
Five Fragments for orchestra, op 42	(1935)
Symphony, No 4 op 43	(1935–6)
Symphony, No 5, op 47	(1937)
Symphony, No 6, op 54	(1939)
Instrumentation of the opera "Boris Godounov", op 58	
Symphony, No 7, op 60	(1941)
Solemn March for wind orchestra	
Concerto for piano, trumpet and string orchestra	

Chamber Music

Trio for violin, cello, and piano, op 8	(1923)

95

Three pieces for cello and piano, op 9   (1923–4)
String Octet, op 11
Sonata for cello and piano, op 40   (1934)
String Quartet, op 49   (1938)
Piano Quintet, op 57   (1940)
Three pieces for violin solo, op 59   (1942)

Pianoforte Music
Eight Preludes, op 2   (1919)
"Three Fantastic Dances", op 5   (1922)
Sonata for two pianos, op 6   (1922)
Sonata, op 12
"Ten Aphorisms", op 13
Twenty-four Preludes, op 34   (1932–3)

Vocal Music
Two Songs for voice and orchestra, text by Krilov, op 4
Six Songs to Japanese texts, op 21
Four Songs, text by Pushkin, op 46
"Oath to the People's Commissar", for chorus and orchestra
                                                (1941)

Opera
"The Nose" after Gogol, op 15   (1927–8)
"Lady Macbeth of Mtensk", op 29   (1930–2)

Ballet
"The Golden Age", op 22   (1929–30)
"The Bolt", op 27   (1930–1)
"Clear Brooks", op 39   (1934)

Theatre Music
Incidental music to the following plays:
  "The Bug", by Mayakovsky, op 19   (1929)
  "The Shot", by Besymensky, op 24   (1929)
  "Virgin Soil", by Gorbenko and Lvov, op 25   (1930)
  "Rule Britannia", by Pyotrovsky, op 28   (1931)
  "Conditionally Killed", by Voyevodin and Riss, op 31 (1931)
  "Hamlet", by Shakespeare, op 32

| "The Human Comedy", after Balzac, op 37 | (1933–4) |
| "Greetings to Spain", by Afinoginev, op 44 | (1936) |

Music for Films

"The New Babylon", op 18	(1928–9)
"Alone", op 26	(1930)
"The Golden Mountains," op 30	(1931)
"The Encounter", op 33	(1932)
"Tale of the Priest and his servant Balba", op 36	
"The Return of Maxine", op 45	(1936–7)
"In the Days of Volochayev", op 48	(1936–7)
"The Viborg District", op 50	(1938)
"Friends", op 51	(1938)
"The Great Citizen", Part I, op 52	(1938)
"The Man with the Gun", op 53	(1938)
"The Great Citizen", Part II, op 55	(1939)
"The Silly Little Mouse", op 56	(1939)

V. V. SHTCHERBATCHEV

Orchestral Music
Four Symphonies

March and Tale	(1913)
Suite from the film "Thunderstorm"	
Two Suites from the film "Peter the Great"	(1939)

Pianoforte Music
Two Sonatas to words by Blok

Vocal Music

| Nonet for voice, flute, harp, string quartet and piano | (1917) |

Opera

| "Anna Kolossova" | (1938) |

Film Music
"Thunderstorm"
"Peter the Great"
"Men of the Baltic"

97

Orchestral Music
Symphony No 1
Symphony No 2
Symphony No 3
Symphony No 4
Suite from the incidental music to the play "Faust and the
    Town", by Lunacharsky   (1928)
"Dramatic Fantasy"
"Heaven and Earth", Symphonic Poem after Bryon
Overture to Maeterlinck's drama "Princess Malen"
Ballet Suite

Chamber Music
String Quartet

Vocal Music
Songs, text by Balmont and Apukhin
Two Song-Cycles, text by Rabindranath Tagore
Five Songs from the Persian
18 Folk-Songs arranged for voice and symphony orchestra

Ballet
"Metamorphoses", after Ovid
"Till Eulenspiegel"   (1938)

Orchestral Music
Symphonic Poem ' To the memory of Twenty-six Commissars"

Chamber Music, Instrumental and Vocal Works
Opera
"Nazar the Brave"
"David Sassunsky"
"The Dawn"

Orchestral Music
Symphony "The Liberation of Byelorussia"   (1929)

Overture and March for wind orchestra
15 Dances for cymbal ensemble

Vocal Music
"The Storm Petrel", for chorus and orchestra, text by M.
    Gorki
"The Avaricious Knight", for bass solo and orchestra, text by
    Pushkin
Choruses and Mass-Songs

Opera
"Mikhas of the Mountain"   (1937–9)

Operetta
"Kitchen of Holiness"

Theatre Music
Incidental music for twenty-two plays for the theatres of Bye-
    lorussian S.S.R.

S. N. VASSILYENKO
Orchestral Music
"Three Bloody Battles", after Tolstoy, op 1
"Epic Poem", op 4   (1900–3)
Symphony, No 1 in A minor, op 10   (1904–6)
Symphonic Poem "The Garden of Death", op 12   (1907–8)
Symphonic Suite "Sappho", op 14   (1909)
"The Flight of the Witches", op 15   (1908–9)
Symphonic Suite "In the Rays of the Sun", op 17   (1910–1)
"Fantastic Waltz", for small orchestra, op 18   (1912)
Suite on lute music of the fourteenth to the seventeenth cen-
    turies, op 24   (1914)
Concerto for violin and orchestra in D minor, op 25   (1910–13)
"Zodiak", Suite on French Themes of the eighteenth century,
    op 27   (1914)
"Exotic Suite", op 29   (1915–6)
Indian Suite from the ballet "Noya", op 42   (1927)
Symphonic Suite from the ballet "Joseph the Beautiful",
    op 41   (1922)
Chinese Suite, op 60   (1928)

99

March of the Red Army, op 64, for wind orchestra   (1929)
Turkmenian Suite, op 68   (1931)
Second Chinese Suite, op 70   (1931)
"Fantasia of Revolutionary Songs of the West", for wind
    orchestra, op 71   (1931)
"Merry-go-round", eight Soviet Dances, op 73   (1932)
Suite "The Soviet East", op 75   (1932)
"Red Army Rhapsody", op 77   (1932)
Cantata, written for the Twentieth Anniversary of the October
    Revolution, op 92   (1937)

Chamber Music
String Quartet in A major, op 3
Sonata for viola and pianoforte, op 46
String Quartet in E minor, op 58
String Quartet on Turkmenian Themes, op 65   (1930)
Japanese Suite, for oboe, clarinet, bassoon, xylophone, and
    pianoforte, op 66a   (1938)
Trio in A major for violin, cello and pianoforte, op 74   (1932)
Chinese Sketches for wood-wind, op 78   (1938)
Quartet on American Themes for wood-wind, op 79   (1938)

Vocal Music
Songs, text by Lermontov, Blok, Balmont, Bryussov, and others
Arrangements of Russian Folk-Songs
Arrangements for voice and various instrument of Indian,
    Cingalese, Maori, Negro melodies, etc.

Opera
"Legend of the Holy City of Kitesh", op 5   (1908)
"The Son of the Sun", op 62   (1929)
"Christopher Columbus", op 80   (1938)
"The Snow Storm" (in collaboration with M. Ashrafi, op 98)(1938)
"The Great Canal", op 101   (1940)
"Suvorov", op 102   (1940–1)

Ballet
"In the Rays of the Sun", op 17   (1925–6)
"Noya", op 42   (1923)
"Joseph the Beautiful", op 50   (1924–5)

"Lola", op 52   (1925–6)
"The Gypsies", after Pushkin, op 90   (1935–6)
"The Princess who was a Frog", op 103   (1941)

A. ZEINALLY

Orchestral Music
Fragments for Symphonic orchestra

Chamber Music
Compositions for violin and cello

Pianoforte Music
Sonata
Nine Fugues

Vocal Music
"Seiran"
"Chadra"
"My Country"
"The Man at the Frontier"
"Araks"
"Daglar"

Theatre Music
Incidental music to eleven plays for the Azerbaijan National
   Theatre